a movable feast
worship for the other six days

terry timm

IMAGINATIONPLUS

Pittsburgh PA

IMAGINATIONPLUS
Pittsburgh, PA
www.imaginationplus.pro

Layout and design by Polome Communications

dedication

To the people of Christ Community Church of the South Hills. Eleven years ago we began an incredible journey of faith together, and it is amazing to step back and see what God has done in us, with us, and through us. Thank you for your sense of adventure and your commitment to be the kind of church that God has called us to be—nothing more and nothing less.

To my wife, Patty. Your presence in my life is a daily reminder of God's goodness and grace. Your partnership, servant heart, and commitment to the well-being of others are shining examples of a Christ-centered life. Thank you for teaching me to feast and helping me taste and see how good God really is.

contents

introduction

I have been serving in the church as a worship leader and pastor for over twenty-five years, and during the course of my ministry there has been an explosion of interest in worship. Thousands of books on worship have been written; a new musical genre called "worship music" has been created, resulting in significant economic gain for many; universities now offer degrees in worship leadership; and if you are unable to devote four years to the subject matter, conferences and training events designed to equip people to experience a deeper level of worship are occurring regularly. Worship is on the rise.

While there is much to celebrate, the renewed focus has brought with it a big downside. Allow me to name it in one word: consumerism. Simply speaking, consumers are people who purchase goods and services to meet a need, either real or perceived. In the most basic of forms, consumption is necessary to human existence. Each and every one of us is a consumer of something. But what happens when consumption goes from necessity to pleasure, from provision to indulgence?

Consumerism. The church is not immune from this mindset. At times, people visit our faith community for one of our Sunday services and say to me, "We are new to the area and are church shopping right now." Now I realize that choosing a local church we can connect with and commit to is a process that calls for much discernment and wisdom. But more often than not, people are checking out the product—the goods and services the church actually provides. For many, the programming offered for children and youth is the key factor. For others, it might be the sense of community, their system of small groups, or the opportunity to be involved in the work of mission and justice in the world. While any of the above factors may influence a decision, in my experience, the overwhelming driver is the Sunday morning worship gathering. People want to be captivated by worship, taught the deep things from Scripture, and ultimately, experience God. When people find a church that offers a product that meets their expectations and desires, their church shopping comes to an end.

The truth is that I have devoted much of my life to designing these kinds of experiences. I am convinced that dynamic and engaging corporate worship is critical to the vitality of a local church. The stakes are high. But if worship is not rightfully understood and practiced, things can go terribly wrong. In a consumer world, worship leaders and preachers are under tremendous pressure to produce high-quality services that keep people coming back, week after week. If a local church does not provide a compelling experience of worship, people may be quick to begin shopping for a better product. This raises an important question: "Are worshippers addicted to the experience of worship, or are we consumed with a deep love and devotion for Jesus Christ?"

My observation is that the culture of worship in the church is producing consumers of worship, rather than people engaged in lifestyles of worship. As I see it, true worship must extend beyond the walls of our corporate gatherings and flow into our everyday, ordinary lives.

An image that fuels my imagination regarding worship is the feast—people coming together to "taste and see the goodness of God." Together we feast on God, through music, prayer, the teaching of the Word, and gathering around the Lord's table to literally taste and see God's goodness.

Our weekly gatherings have become spiritual high points that produce an emotional and spiritual high that fills people and carries them through their week. And their desperate hope is that they will have enough fuel in their spiritual tanks to make it to the next Sunday when they can fill up again. I see this heartbreaking scenario play out regularly in the lives of countless followers of Jesus, and it has prompted me to ask this question: "What if the people of God came into our Sunday gatherings energized because they have experienced 'the feast of worship' during the other six days of the week?"

You see, God intended worship to be a movable feast— something we carry into our everyday, ordinary lives. The activities of worship experienced in our corporate gatherings (praise, prayers, confession, affirmations of faith, acts of generosity, and hearing the Word of God) are practices that can connect us deeply with God throughout the entire week.

Eugene Peterson's translation of Romans 12 captures the everyday, ordinary nature of worship:

> "So here's what I want you to do, God helping you: Take your everyday, ordinary life—your sleeping, eating,

going-to-work, and walking-around life—and place it
before God as an offering." (Romans 12:1, The Message)

What if the people of God embraced this text, praying that it would be not only words printed on a page but a truth that becomes a way of life? What might worship look like in the places we live, learn, work, serve, and play?

I see educators, healthcare providers, attorneys, and people in information technology and human resources offering their work back to God as worship.

I see a transformed marketplace, as workers envision their labors as embodied benedictions and their contributions to the common good as lived prayers of blessing and peace.

I see students diligently pursuing their coursework not just as pathways to successful careers, but as acts of worship as they offer their studies back to God.

I see neighborhood coaches who believe that our play matters to God, using their leadership skills to teach girls and boys values like commitment and teamwork, and that when we use our bodies in the manner God intended, we honor our Creator and bring him praise.

I see people digging wells in East Africa, doing Hurricane Katrina relief work in the Gulf Coast, and serving low-income homeowners in our cities. They do so as more than merely social action but as labors of love, offered to God as acts of worship.

This is the vision that has motivated me to write this book. My heart is to empower the people of God to move beyond a consumer approach to worship, and *A Movable Feast: Worship for the Other Six Days* is a practical guide for anyone who desires to do so. In the pages that follow, you will discover that the kind of worship that pleases God extends beyond the walls of the church and connects to God's redemptive purposes in the world today.

The book begins with some personal stories that will help you develop a keener awareness of God's presence and activity in the everyday, ordinary events of life. Growing in our capacity to see God at work all around us can lead to a deeper reverence that fuels a life of worship. After sharing my definition of worship, I will explore the connection between worship, mission, and justice. As well, I propose that our worship involves work, and quite often that work is challenging because our world is fractured and things simply are not the way they ought to be.

Finally, I suggest that worship is the eternal activity, and I sketch out what worship in the new creation might look like. If heavenly worship as a non-stop sing-along with harps and angelic choruses does not captivate your imagination, you are not alone. My hope is that a robust understanding of how a life of worship might unfold in the future will build a sense of anticipation within you.

Before we get started, here is one more observation: Christians have a fascination with worship leaders. More often than not these leaders are gifted musicians, skillful in moving people through the power of song. Being a musician myself, I have a big place in my heart for people who lead worship musically. As important as music is, if the people of God are going to move beyond consumerist worship, we need to be captivated by a new worship leader. The leader who should be setting the pace is none other than Jesus. By following Jesus, the one who offered his life back to God for the life of the world, we can participate more fully in the feast of worship in every dimension of life.

Thanks for joining me on this journey. May the words that follow inform your mind, engage your soul, and empower you to become a more wholehearted worshipper.

taste and see the goodness of God

Open your mouth and taste.
Open your eyes and see how good God is.
—Psalm 34:8 (The Message)

During her junior year of college, my daughter Hannah had the opportunity to study abroad for a semester in Florence, Italy. Who could imagine a better place for an art major to study art than in the cradle of creativity that produced some of the finest artists of the Renaissance such as Michelangelo and Botticelli? While Hannah was in Italy, we stayed connected via Skype, and whenever we talked, I was sure to ask her what new things she was experiencing as part of her art education. As a parent, I wanted to make sure she was squeezing every last drop out of this very rich (and might I add expensive) educational opportunity. In each conversation, I inquired about the latest gallery she visited, the new artists and techniques she was being introduced to, or some new factoid about art history. To her credit, Hannah was always good to oblige me with a quick update about her art experiences. But the energy in her voice always increased when the conversation moved toward the topic of food. Comments like, "Dad, let me tell you about the great market I visited," or "I had the best pasta ever in this little open-air café," and "Over the weekend, I took a cooking class where I learned how to prepare perfect tiramisu," reminded me that, while her time in Florence was designed to enhance her knowledge and experience of art, Hannah was equally captivated by the rich culture, gift, and experience that surrounds the table.

Open your mouth and taste. Open your eyes and see. See how good God really is.

I love the way Eugene Peterson takes the familiar words from Psalm 34, "O taste and see that the Lord is good," and brings them to life in a fresh way. When is the last time you opened your mouth and tasted the goodness of God? Perhaps it was a purple grape that burst with flavor as you bit into it. Maybe it was the fresh mango salsa that was served alongside a pulled pork sandwich, or the slice of coconut cream pie that was the perfect conclusion to a fine meal. Maybe it was a plate of injera and shiro wat (a common Ethiopian meal), a savory couscous dish, or a hot dog with the works from a street vendor. Each of these foods, in their own unique fashion, are masterful in their own right—each one an opportunity to taste and see the goodness of God. But there is a big difference between simply beholding the beauty of something and actually partaking of it. Every day, in a sense, God sets the table and invites us to not only consider how good God is, but also engage in God's goodness. Allow me to take you to a few of the places where I have discovered this reality.

Open your mouth and taste. Open your eyes and see. See how good God really is.

Early in my ministry, my first congregation occasionally relieved me of my Sunday morning leadership responsibilities and encouraged me to visit other local churches. Part of this plan was for me to learn from other worshipping communities and bring back what might be transferable from their experience to our congregation. But a significant aspect of this time and space was to simply nurture and feed my own relationship with God (a wise move on the part of this congregation, I might add).

One Sunday morning, I had the opportunity to worship in an Episcopal church. The rector of this church was well-known both locally and globally for his teaching ministry and evangelistic crusades. The church was a stunning place to worship. The sanctuary was a place of beauty, space that had been carefully designed to create a sense of awe and reverence. This was my first opportunity to participate in the Anglican liturgy. I was unfamiliar with the flow of the liturgy, the changing body postures, and the movement between sitting, kneeling, and standing. Many of the spoken prayers, although old, were new to me. Needless to say, it was extremely different from my normal Sunday morning worship experience.

While it was inspiring to hear the word of God proclaimed by the rector of this congregation, the climax of the gathering came near the end of the liturgy as we were invited to receive the Eucharist. The practice of this congregation was to invite people to walk to the front of the sanctuary and kneel at the rail in front of the communion table. There the priest came and offered to each of us the body of Christ. Then the chalice was offered to us, the common cup from which we had the opportunity to open our mouths and drink the cup of salvation.

I grew up in the Methodist Church, which, if you are not aware, uses grape juice for communion. This Episcopal church did not use grape juice. As I opened my mouth and drank deeply from the chalice, I was surprised by the goodness of God in a fresh and memorable way. In that moment, as the wine invaded my body and warmed my insides, I experienced in the depth of my being an assurance that there is a good God who loves me so much that God's one and only Son would come to pay the price for my redemption.

Open your mouth and taste. Open your eyes and see. See how good God really is.

I was on a trip to upstate New York, headed there for a personal retreat and some quiet time and space. Cruising east along I-90 on a glorious autumn day, I was simply enjoying the wide open space of the road. As I entered the stunningly beautiful Lake Chautauqua area, I turned up the volume of my car's sound system and began rocking out to the CD that was playing at the time.

The song I was listening to declared that God was indeed the God of all creation and a God of wonders. The music spoke of the beauty of God and that which God has created—the water, the mountains, the sea—everything God has created does its part by responding to the Creator with worship. In that moment, at a cruising speed of at least sixty-five miles an hour and with the volume of my sound system maxed out, God whispered to me, "Terry, turn the CD player off. Open your eyes and see. See what I have created and worship me." Even though I was driving through one of the most beautiful places in the world, I was oblivious to the beauty and majesty of God, because I was more captivated by the music that spoke of God than by God himself.

Responding to the prompting of the Spirit, I stopped my car, opened my eyes, and worshipped the God of all creation.

Open your mouth and taste. Open your eyes and see. See how good God really is.

Not long ago, I bumped into Courtney. It had been quite some time seen I had seen Courtney and her mother, and it pleased me to learn that she had recently turned sixteen and successfully passed her driver's examination. Based on our brief conversation, Courtney seemed to be thriving and living the typically teenage life—at times making her mother extremely proud and at times making her mother extremely crazy.

I will never forget the first time I met Courtney. I was introduced to her in the neonatal intensive-care unit of Children's Hospital in Pittsburgh. She entered the world over two months prematurely and at the time of her birth weighed less than two pounds. She was so small that if I could have held her, she would easily have fit in the palm of my hand. Teetering on the brink between life and death, Courtney spent many weeks in the NICU. Would her lungs develop properly? Would her heart keep beating? Would her immune system be strong enough to fight off infection? Would her vision and hearing be compromised? Would her intestinal system enable her to digest food?

Psalm 139 reminds us that we are "fearfully and wonderfully created by God." Seeing Courtney after all these years brought that truth home to me in a powerful way. As I walked away from our encounter, I brushed away tears of joy from my eyes; thanks to the wonders of medical technology and the prayers of God's people, Courtney not only survived, but today she thrives.

Open your mouth and taste. Open your eyes and see. See how good God really is.

A few summers ago, my oldest nephew was married. Adam and his bride selected a spectacular venue for their wedding, a beautiful garden setting called Phipps Conservatory. While a rainstorm briefly threatened the outdoor ceremony, in the nick of time the clouds parted, the rains stopped, and the sun began to shine. Against the brilliant backdrop of the city skyline and the sounds of a string quartet, Adam and Kate pledged their love and commitment to one another. After the ceremony, as family and friends, we feasted on an amazing assortment of food, celebrating the gift of love long into the night.

While it was a beautiful occasion, throughout the celebration there was an ache in my heart; someone significant was missing. When Adam was a small boy, his father was on a business trip to Chicago. Finishing his business earlier than expected, Randy hurried to O'Hare Airport and talked his way onto an earlier flight back to Pittsburgh. Being the homebody and family man that he was, I can imagine how thrilled he must have been to be able to return home and spend time with his wife and three young children. However, this family reunion would not take place. Just five minutes from landing in Pittsburgh, US Airways Flight 427 experienced catastrophic mechanical failure, crashing to the ground and killing all 132 people onboard.

My brother-in-law's absence at the wedding reminded me of the stark reality that many festive occasions leave a bittersweet taste. Baptism and birthday parties, graduation ceremonies and high school reunions—whatever the occasion may be—there will be empty seats, as fathers, mothers, sisters, brothers, husbands, wives, and friends are missing from the table. In the midst of these gatherings, unanswerable questions arise: "If God is love, why would God allow an airplane to fall out of the sky? If God is strong, why couldn't God prevent it?" We wonder, is it possible to believe, let alone experience, the goodness of God?

In the midst of sadness and sorrow, we celebrate what is, acknowledge what is not, and anticipate what will be. We feast on the hope that there is coming a day when sadness or sorrow will be no more, and we cling to the promise that one day every tear will be wiped away.

Open your mouth and taste. Open your eyes and see. See how good God really is.

My wife and I enjoy traveling together, and one of our favorite places to visit is the city of Toronto, Ontario, located north of the U.S. border. We love the eclectic vibe of the city—the sights, sounds, and smells, and the fact that on any given city block, you will find a cacophony of languages being spoken.

Years ago, during one of our visits, we were able to secure tickets to see the musical version of the Lion King. As the parent of four children, I have watched the Lion King video countless times, memorized most of the dialogue, and been captivated by Elton John's memorable melodic hooks. In my opinion, however, nothing quite compares to the stage version of the Lion King.

I recall sitting in the theater, anticipating my first experience of the musical version. The house lights dimmed, and the opening "Circle of Life" scene began with a joyous procession of gifted actors and actresses portraying the animals of the Serengeti, each festooned with amazing colors, fabrics, and textures. As the animal kingdom entered the theater, slowly moving through the aisles and ultimately converging onto the stage in a finely choreographed dance, my eyes were opened. I felt the rhythm and heard the harmonies, and I saw in a fresh way just how good and creative God actually is. And if the wild beasts can lift up their voices in such soulful fashion, who am I to withhold my song and dance from my Creator?

Open your mouth and taste. Open your eyes and see. See how good God really is.

A few summers ago, I traveled to Kampala, Uganda, to participate in a training conference for pastors and church leaders from seven East African nations. Having the opportunity and privilege to invest in the lives of these faithful and committed church leaders and to learn from them as well has been one of the highlights of my life.

Just days before our international team arrived, the Ugandan government made a decision to evict over 30,000 people who lived in the Nakawa Estate. Before your imagination gets carried away, the word "estate" was simply formal Ugandan terminology (left behind by the British) for the many neighborhoods in and around Kampala that were little more than urban slums. Because the Nakawa Estate was located in close proximity to the city center, in the eyes of the government it was prime real estate. In the name of economic and urban development, bulldozers leveled the entire community: in a matter of days, homes, places of business, and yes, even churches were demolished.

One afternoon, our team traveled to Nakawa and stood in the rubble that once was the New Life Baptist Church. Pastor Peter and his wife Rose had given ten years of their lives to building that church, serving the poor, and sharing the gospel with the people who called Nakawa home. As they shared their story, my heart was captivated by their commitment and passion. And my heart was broken as they shared how in a matter of minutes everything was completely destroyed. Nothing remained but piles of brick and other materials the scavengers had not yet carried away.

Yet as they spoke, their faith was palpable and their conviction strong: the One who built their church would not allow human instruments of destruction to prevail. Their church was more than a building, and this act of injustice could not and would not stop them from serving the needs of their displaced congregation.

As we walked through the grounds in silence, in the midst of the devastation, we found a portion of the Bible that had been left behind: "The grass withers and the flowers fall, but the word of our God endures forever" (Isaiah 40:8). These words reminded me of the faithfulness of God and that in spite of any circumstance, the promises of God are sure and certain.

Open your mouth and taste. Open your eyes and see. See how good God really is.

I had gathered with a group of close friends and family members in a sold-out Mellon Arena in Pittsburgh for a long-awaited appearance by the band U2. The occasion was a stop on the Elevation tour, and as a latecomer to the music and message of U2, this was my first time experiencing the band in concert. A U2 event is rich with drama, spectacle, and theater, each moment having been carefully and thoughtfully crafted to engage the audience on multiple levels.

Near the end of the concert, there appeared onstage a colorful backdrop that, upon closer inspection, was actually made up of flags from the nations of the world. One by one, the flags descended and rotated in a digital dance around the stage. In that moment, something transcendent occurred as The Edge begin to play that magical, mystical guitar riff that serves as the unmistakable prelude to the song "Where the Streets Have No Name." In the midst of family and friends, surrounded by sisters and brothers in Christ, and in a multitude of people unknown to me but deeply known by God, for a few moments I realized that there is indeed coming a day when the streets will have no name. There is coming a day when all the peoples of the earth, all of the nations, will live as one—as God's people. In the midst of that gathering, I opened my mouth and tasted, opened my ears and heard, opened my eyes and saw how good God is.

Open your mouth and taste. Open your eyes and see. See how good God really is.

Over the course of my ministry, I have had opportunities to witness the work of God in a number of different countries around the globe. One of the most impactful experiences was participating in a pastors' vision trip to Kenya and Ethiopia with World Vision, an international aid and development organization. As part of this trip, a small team of us traveled to a remote region of Ethiopia known as Guraghe. There we observed the incredible work of World Vision and saw firsthand how meeting the physical needs of people—from clean water and food security to the role of education and compassionate care in preventing the spread of HIV and AIDS—opens the door to give testimony to the good news of Jesus Christ.

One Sunday morning, our team gathered with a congregation that met in a simply constructed, minimally furnished building. The small space was filled beyond capacity, and in fact, many gathered outside the building and joined in the worship through the many openings in the walls. There was a strong sense of anticipation at what might transpire in this gathering. Needless to say it was quite humorous for the locals to watch our group try to find the unique nuances of the Ethiopian rhythms and melodies.

At one point during worship, I had the opportunity to pick up a guitar, and our team led the congregation in singing a simple song of worship that speaks of the people of God falling down and laying their crowns at the feet of Jesus. While the language barriers made it difficult to translate all the words, a beautiful sound emerged when Americans and Ethiopians together, each in our own language declared this heavenly chorus: "Holy, holy, holy is the Lord."

Open your mouth and taste. Open your eyes and see. See how good God really is.

In his book *For All God's Worth: True Worship and the Calling of the Church*, N. T. Wright raises three significant questions: "What is the most beautiful thing you experienced this week? What does this beauty do to you? What does this beauty call out of you?"

And Wright continues:

> *Gratitude—of course; delight—yes, naturally; a sense of awe—well, perhaps; a sense of longing for something beyond, something just out of reach—quite possibly, though if your experience of beauty was the smell of a good meal I hope it did not stay out of reach for long. What about worship? Does beauty call out worship from you?*

In the spirit of Wright's questions, would you pause for a moment and ask yourself these questions: When is the last time you opened your mouth and tasted the goodness of God? When is the last time you opened your eyes and saw how good God is?

17

What did this experience evoke within you? Did it call forth your worship?

Each day, in the ordinary and not so ordinary moments of life, in our deepest joys and heartfelt sorrows, we have the opportunity to taste and see the goodness of God. Every day we have the opportunity to respond to God's goodness with awe, gratitude, delight, reverence, and yes, even worship. In the next chapter, we will explore the wonder of worship and the invitation from God to come to God's table and feast.

an invitation to feast

"To everything there is a time and season."
—*Ecclesiastes 3:1*

One of my neighbors has a venti dream (Starbucks fans know what I am talking about) for her life, a dream hidden in the deep place of her heart. Ann possesses a strong gift of hospitality, and on numerous occasions, I have personally benefitted from her wonderful skills as a cook, baker, and hostess. If Ann could find the financial backing, she would love to open her own catering business. One day in conversation, Ann mentioned to me that she already has a name selected for her business, confidently declaring that it would be called "A Movable Feast."

Intrigued by the name, I researched the phrase "a movable feast" and discovered that Ann is not the only one with this idea. All across the country, there are catering companies that have taken on that very same name, "A Movable Feast." These businesses will come to your home or office and deliver the finest of foods. Many of them will prepare baskets that you can take with you on a picnic or other outing. On any given day, wherever life may take you, you can participate in a delicious feast.

The concept of "a movable feast" was not unique to my friend or in fact to any of the numerous catering companies that integrate those words into their business. *A Movable Feast* happens to be the title of Ernest Hemingway's final book, a memoir that explores his experience of Paris during the final days of his life. One line in the book captures the essence of the movable feast: "If you are lucky enough to have lived in Paris as a young man, then wherever you go for the rest of your life, it stays with you. For Paris is a movable feast."

Imagine the scene: the Eiffel Tower, the chiming of church bells, the smell of freshly baked croissants, all combining to create the vibe and the ambience of the metropolis known as the "City of Light." Hemingway believed that if a person were fortunate to have this type of rich, sensual experience early in life, the experience would be carried into the rest of his or her life. Paris is a movable feast.

Now I realize that Hemingway, despite his literary brilliance, was not a person whose lifestyle you would necessarily want to emulate. As my son reminded me, "Dad, Hemingway was a freak—a bizarre, strange, and broken man." But I believe there is great power in his idea of bringing rich experiences from our past into our present and future experience.

Truth be told, neither my friend Ann, the catering companies, nor even Hemingway himself were the originators of this expression, "a movable feast." Long before Hemingway or a host of caterers appropriated the term, the church of Jesus Christ used the phrase to describe a sacred day in the liturgical church calendar. A movable feast was a day of remembrance and celebration that was not fixed or anchored to any one particular day of the calendar. Follow me into a tale of two calendars to better understand this.

A Tale of Two Calendars

Have you ever awakened in the morning and during those first moments of pre-coffee consciousness wondered, "What day is it?" For a person of faith, this can be quite a profound question.

For example, as I am writing this sentence, my iCal app tells me that it is Monday, June 21, and for this designation, I owe a debt of gratitude to both Julius Caesar and Pope Gregory XIII. The Julian calendar, a reform of the Roman calendar, was first introduced by Julius Caesar in 46 BC. It has a regular year of 365 days divided into twelve months, and a leap day is added to February every four years. As a result, the Julian year is on average 365.25 days long.

The Julian calendar basically kept people on the same calendar page until the sixteenth century, when Pope Gregory XIII introduced the Gregorian calendar to the world through a papal decree. Gregory's primary intention was to restore the calendar so that seasonal events critical for the calculation of Easter dates would be back in their "proper places" and would be prevented from ever again being moved.

The need for the Gregorian reform emerged from the fact that the Julian calendar system assumed the time between vernal equinoxes, which mark the first day of spring, to be 365.25 days, when in actuality it is eleven minutes less. Now eleven minutes might not be a major problem if you happen to be late for lunch with a friend, but from a larger framework of time, the accumulated error over the years was significant. Due mostly to this discrepancy, between AD 325 and the time of Gregory's edict in 1582, the vernal equinox had moved ten days earlier in the calendar, now occurring around March 11. Since the vernal equinox was directly connected to the celebration of Easter, one of the high holy days in the life of the church, the Roman Catholic Church undertook the reform in the calendar. While you and I may sync our technological toys on a regular basis, this reform by the church could be viewed as the first technological sync—by dropping ten days, the church realigned the calendar and seasons.

Change like this is not always embraced. As a result of the Protestant Reformation, many Western European countries did not initially follow the Gregorian reform, choosing instead to maintain the older systems. However, necessity eventually won the day, and most countries went on to adopt the Gregorian calendar.

People of Two Calendars

In reality, people of faith organize their lives around two calendars. We use the Gregorian calendar—the first calendar—to orient our daily lives. Meetings, dentist appointments, soccer games, birthdays, and anniversaries all revolve around the first calendar. But there is a second calendar that we need to wrap our lives around, and this method of orienting our lives is known as the liturgical calendar. Just as June 21 marks the longest day of the year and the beginning of summer, there are mile markers along the liturgical way reminding us that the Lord we worship and serve is indeed a God whose glory, majesty, and purposes in our world are revealed through seasons.

While the first calendar begins with a New Year's celebration on January 1, the liturgical year commences with the first Sunday in the season of Advent, a season consisting of the four Sundays before Christmas. Advent prepares us for Christmas, which in turn gives way to Epiphany and ultimately Lent, Easter, Pentecost, and Ordinary Time. Each liturgical season reminds us of the activity of God on behalf of humanity, as well as the responsibility and privilege that belong to the people of God to partner with God in the work of redemption in our world. While the life cycle of the Jewish community of faith centers around the movement of the exodus from Egypt, the Christian year is oriented around the life and ministry of Jesus. The sequence of events from Advent to Resurrection Sunday is a yearlong journey during which worshippers long for the coming of Messiah, kneel at the manger, listen and learn of the kingdom of God, walk the streets of Jerusalem, stand at the foot of the cross, journey to the tomb, and witness the resurrection! The rest of the church year provides opportunity to reflect on the meaning of the coming of Jesus and the commission to his people to be a light to the world, a city set on a hill, in and through the power of the Holy Spirit.

Allow me to pause and define a term here. The word liturgy[1] means "the work of the people." Throughout history, the community of faith understood that worship was a gift in which they were called to fully participate and engage. The liturgical calendar provided a framework and structure for the people of God to participate in this work of worship on a regular basis and in rhythmic fashion. The good news is that the people of God have historically engaged in the work of worship and marked

---

[1] Liturgy (*leitourgia*) is a Greek composite word originally meaning a public duty or responsibility, a service to the state undertaken by a citizen. Its elements are *leitos* (from *leos* = *laos*, people) meaning "public," and *ergo* meaning "to do." From this we have *leitourgos*, a person who performs a public duty.

important milestones along the way through the celebration of feast days.

In the liturgical life of the church, there are both fixed feasts and movable feasts. We are all familiar with a fixed feast. Do you ever stop and wonder what day we will celebrate Christmas this year? Of course not—there is no need for speculation because we all know Christmas is anchored to December 25. Mark it down. It is fixed. The church (and our culture in general) has latched onto that day, and therefore it has become a fixed feast.

We are also familiar with a movable feast. What celebration and feast moves from year to year? Easter. The church has established a complex formula based upon the phases of the moon that determines when Easter will be celebrated. Moving from year to year, Easter can occur as early as March 22 and as late as April 25. Therefore, Easter is considered a movable feast. In the liturgical calendar, there are a number of feasts directly connected to Easter. For example, the celebration of the ascension of Jesus and the day of Pentecost both move in the calendar based upon their relationship to the date of Easter.

Feasting has historically been an important practice for the people of God. For over two thousand years of church history, the faithful have gravitated toward remembering the goodness and graciousness of God by eating and celebrating together. Feasting is not unique to the church. As the narrative of God's salvation history unfolds in the Old Testament, we discover that God built into the fabric of the Hebraic community the opportunity and occasion to feast.

It is important to remember that, particularly in ancient history (and even today in many developing parts of the world), food was a rare commodity, and good food was even rarer. So God built into the life cycle of the community of faith regular and rhythmic opportunities to gather together and feast. Within the Jewish community, people would leave their homes and communities and travel to the holy city of Jerusalem, and there they would celebrate. They would bring and sacrifice the best they had to offer. They would eat in remembrance of the goodness of God who delivered them from the bondage of slavery they experienced in Egypt. And as salvation history moved forward, those who first trusted in Jesus as Messiah feasted and celebrated on the wondrous grace and provision of God found in Christ.

However, long before the liturgical calendar came into existence and even before the Hebrew community began to celebrate together, feasting and communion were already occurring. It was taking place in the very life of the triune God.

The Divine Dance

God has existed eternally as Father, Son, and Holy Spirit. The life of God is rooted in relationship, and understanding the depth of this communion is essential to understanding God's nature and being. We do not think of God as three separate entities who happen to be in relationship with one another (i.e., the Father has a relationship with the Son, the Son has a relationship with the Spirit). Rather, the relationships themselves are the very essence and being of God. The early church fathers used a particular word to describe the relational dynamics within the life of the triune God. *Perichoresis,* or circle dance, first appears in the writings of Gregory of Nazianzus (AD 329–389) and was later explored more fully by John of Damascus (AD 676–749).

Imagine a Middle Eastern feast. A host would plan and prepare a great feast, extending invitations to many. The host would also make arrangements for musical entertainment, as singing and dancing were an integral part of any celebration. In the midst of the feast, while the guests dined on the finest of foods, the host would signal the bandleader. As the music filled the room, guests would rise from their feasting, and a dance would begin to unfold. One by one people would join in the movement and energy of the dance until all the members of the party had taken their place.

This image of perichoresis was adopted by the early church fathers and used to help God's people better comprehend the life of God. The image of the divine dance is not so much about the dancers as it is about the patterns of the dance itself—an interweaving of divine motion, movement, and energy. In the circle dance, the intertwined movements signify deep connection; the dancers not only move around each other, they penetrate into one another, reflecting a tremendous sense of relational depth. In God's economy, the persons of the Trinity relate intimately, moving within and through each other in a dance above all dances. When we speak of the parts played by the divine persons in this circle dance, the Son indwells the Father, the Father contains the Son, and the Spirit fills the Father.

One theologian, Paul Fiddes, likens this to a progressive dance. By this he means a dance where the participants move outside of the original circle, expanding it by inviting others to join in the pattern of movement.[2] So it is with the divine dance. The divine dance of the Father, the Son, and the Holy Spirit draws and invites us into the energizing and invigorating movement. Perichoresis tells the story that invites us to enter the

---

[2] Paul Fiddes, *Participating in God: A Pastoral Doctrine of the Trinity* (Louisville: Westminster John Knox Press, January 2001), 79.

personal movements of the love within the divine community of God.

This celebration is all about the gift of grace. Anne Lamott describes this gift: "Grace meets us where we are, but it does not leave us there."[3] Grace invites us deeper into the life of God. And it is in Christ that we find and receive the gift of grace.

In speaking of the connection between grace, movement, and worship, James Torrance, in his masterful book *Worship, Community and the Triune Grace of God*, writes:

> *But not only is that grace applicable to our salvation, the forgiveness of sins, our life with God after we die. But in Christ we begin to experience the gift of grace as a movement. Not only God's movement toward us, but our movement toward God in Christ. ... Jesus lifts us out of ourselves to participate in the very life and communion with God. That life of communion for which we were created. We are in Christ, and if we are in Christ, it means we are where Jesus is.[4]*

And where is Jesus? He is eternally and continually engaging in the divine dance, in communion with the Father and with the Spirit. If we are in Christ, we are there as well.

As this feasting takes place, and as this dancing and celebrating are going on, God invites you and me to join in. It's a party, a 24/7 celebration! I love the way Anglican priest and author Maggi Dawn describes this activity:

---

[3] Anne Lamott, *Traveling Mercies: Some Thoughts on Faith* (New York: Anchor Books, 2000), 143.

[4] James B. Torrance, *Worship, Community and the Triune God of Grace* (Downers Grove: InterVarsity Press, 1997), 22.

The call to worship is therefore an invitation to join in with God's party. Worship is already underway. Come and join in if you like. No need to DO anything. If you want to dance you can dance, but if you want to sit for a while and let it all wash over you and through you, you can do that too. Of course, at some point you will get drawn into the giving, communicating, adoring, loving activity, but there's no pressure, because God doesn't need your little mite of energy to drive the worship machine.[5]

Worship is occurring right now. And God says, "Come. Feast with us. Dance with us."

And yet there is more. New Testament scholar Edith Humphreys, in her book *Ecstasy and Intimacy,* takes this idea to an even deeper level. She describes the divine movement and activity as follows:

The word that St. John and others use to describe this mystic phenomenon is not the Greek word for dance (perichoresis, with a short o). ... But for our Triune God, another word is used (perichoresis, with a long o): this is a word that implies a far deeper spiritual intercommunion than a mere inter-weaving dance! We are here on the border of mystery, or as the unfriendly Edward Gibson once remarked, 'at the deepest and darkest corner of the whole theological abyss.'...To think further upon the divine concourse is to evoke a spiritual blush, indeed, to tread on blasphemy; our search for a

---

[5] Maggi Dawn, "Ten Minutes on the Trinity," *Maggi Dawn* (blog), July 18, 2004, http://maggidawn.typepad.com/maggidawn/2004/07/ten_minutes_on_.html.

*dim analogy in human experience will lead us far
beyond the reserve of dance.*[6]

Can I ask you a personal question? When is the last time you contemplated worship and discovered that you were blushing?

The Feast of God

So often when it comes to worship, we think we have to do something. But God invites us to simply come and join in the celebration that is already occurring. Come and participate in this glorious feast that God has prepared. What does the party of God look like, sound like, smell like, taste like, and feel like? How might we envision the scene? How might we experience it?

This book is entitled *A Movable Feast* as it is rooted in the deep reality that right now, even as you are reading these words, there is a grand feast being celebrated in the heavenly places. God the Father, God the Son, and God the Holy Spirit are feasting together. The triune God is celebrating the divine life together. One of the most vivid Scriptural images that captures the feasting nature of God is found in Isaiah 25. This beautiful scene is more than a future event we are anticipating; this future reality invites us to live in and experience the present in a profoundly different way. The reality is this feast that is occurring right now in eternity can be experienced in real time as well. The feast that is anchored in the eternal also moves from place to place and through time and space. In this very moment, we can come to the table and experience communion with God the Father, the Son, and the Holy Spirit.

---

[6] Edith M. Humphrey, *Ecstasy and Intimacy: When the Holy Spirit Meets the Human Spirit* (Grand Rapids: Wm. B. Eerdmans Publishing Company, 2005), 92–93.

> *On this mountain the LORD Almighty will prepare a feast of rich food for all peoples, a banquet of aged wine—the best of meats and the finest of wines. On this mountain he will destroy the shroud that enfolds all peoples, the sheet that covers all nations; he will swallow up death forever. The Sovereign LORD will wipe away the tears from all faces; he will remove his people's disgrace from all the earth. The LORD has spoken. In that day they will say, "Surely this is our God; we trusted in him, and he saved us. This is the LORD, we trusted in him; let us rejoice and be glad in his salvation." (Isaiah 25:6-9)*

What a beautiful and compelling picture. There is coming a day when the Lord Almighty will prepare a feast of rich foods— the finest of meats and the finest of wines—for all people. Isn't that a wonderful phrase? For all people—not just a select few.

On that day, and on that mountain, God promises to destroy the shroud that enfolds all the people. This shroud is a symbol describing everything that holds them back, everything that confuses and dampens their life and their experience. God will destroy it by swallowing up death forever, wiping away tears, and removing humanity's disgrace from all the earth.

There's a full recognition by the prophet Isaiah that the people are disgraceful. As we read this text, we need to remember that we as well have done disgraceful things. We sin against God, against one another, and against the creation. Like the people of Israel, we are a disgraced and shamed people. But the promise is that God, at this feast, is going to wipe it all away. And in that day we will say, "Surely this is our God; we trusted him and he saved us. This is the Lord, we trusted in him; let us rejoice and be glad in his salvation."

Here Is the New There

Are you familiar with the word "snowclone"? According to Wikipedia, "a snowclone conveys information by using a familiar verbal formula and the cultural knowledge of the audience." Perhaps the best-known example of a snowclone is the phrase, "_____ is the new black." This phrase was created to indicate the sudden popularity or versatility of an idea at the expense of the popularity of a second idea. "X is the new Y." For example, "forty is the new thirty" or "small is the next big."

Try this one on for size: "Here is the new there; now is the new then."[7] As we consider the vision of Isaiah 25, here becomes the new there, and now becomes the new then because the future, in a sense, is already occurring. Through Jesus and being where he is, God's people are already communing and living into the present life of God. While we can and should certainly anticipate the day when the feast of God will be fully actualized, right now the feast becomes to us a movable feast as the future is being dragged into this present moment.

If you looked in my wallet right now, you would discover that I am carrying around with me a number of gift cards for local coffee shops and restaurants. Gift cards are great because they free me up from having to worry about having cash or a credit card on hand. In many cases they are actually gifts, meaning that someone else has already paid the price and I now can eat and drink freely.

Isaiah 25 is a gift card for the people of God. No expiration date, no unique exclusions, no locations off limits. You can use it

---

[7] My thanks to Rob Bell who uses this phrase as the title of a chapter in his book *Love Wins: A Book About Heaven, Hell, and the Fate of Every Person Who Ever Lived* (New York: HarperOne, 2011).

anytime and in any place, because God's table is always open—in the places where we live, learn, work, serve, and play. Look closely at the fine print on the card, for it says something like this: "You are invited to participate in God's feast anytime and anywhere."

One of the richest learning experiences of my life came during a season of graduate study at Northern Theological Seminary outside of Chicago. During my course of study there, I had the opportunity to take a number of courses with one of the foremost authorities on worship, Dr. Robert Webber. Bob, as his students lovingly knew him, was a true gift to the church, having authored over thirty books on worship. Bob was quite a character, a hippie of sorts with his trademark long, flowing, gray hair. He had not a musical bone in his body, and he was not concerned about appearances or up on pop culture. But he loved God, loved to worship, and loved to invite others to come to the table and feast.

When I was in Chicago doing my class work, students would typically study together during the day, from early in the morning until around five o'clock in the afternoon. We would break for the day, have a quick dinner, and then spend the rest of the evening preparing for the next day's content. Whenever I had a class with Bob, however, the daily routine had a much different twist to it. At the end of the day, instead of retreating to our rooms, we would spend our evenings in community together at the lovely home of Bob and his wife. Welcomed into their spacious kitchen, we spent hours cooking, laughing, eating rich food, and drinking good wine together. We feasted together as God's people.

Bob Webber was obsessed with a deep love for Jesus. Living out his faith within the context of a liturgical tradition, he had a deep appreciation for the fixed feasts of the church. But just as important, Bob understood that worship was not confined to a fixed time or place: every moment in time and every space and place become opportunities to approach the table of the Lord and feast. While his earthly existence was cut short by cancer, I know with certainty that, at this moment, Bob Webber is feasting at the table with our brothers and sisters in Christ who have left this dimension and are now living in the fullness of the divine community of God. We who carry on in the here and now do so in anticipation of that day as we live, act, and worship.

In 1998, Brian Doerksen wrote the classic worship song, "Come, Now Is the Time to Worship." Many churches use this song in their service of worship as a sung call to worship. Considering the lyrical content, that makes perfect sense. However, imagine moving the song to the end of a worship gathering and leveraging it as a way of sending the people of God out into the world as worshippers—as a way of taking the feast from here to there:

> *Come, now is the time to worship*
> *Now is the time to give your heart*
> *Come, just as you are to worship*
> *Just as you are before your God*
> *One day every tongue will confess you are God*
> *One day every knee will bow, still the greatest treasure*
> *Remains for those who gladly choose you now*
> *Willingly we choose to surrender our lives*
> *Willingly our knee will bow*
> *With all our heart, soul, mind and strength*
> *We gladly choose you now*[8]

---

[8] Brian Doerksen, 1998 Vineyard Songs (UK/Eire).

Worship is a grand invitation that contains an incredible promise: those who willingly choose to accept the invitation to feast at God's table will receive the treasure of participation in the very life of God. We now turn our attention to defining worship and exploring the opportunities, both fixed and movable, to join the divine dance and participate in the feast. Here is the new there; now is the new then. And now is the time to worship.

what is worship?

The only real fall of man is his noneucharistic life
in a noneucharistic world.

—*Alexander Schmemann*

The term "comfort food" has taken on new meaning and significance in our expanding culture of food. Technically speaking, comfort foods are simple and familiar meals that are either prepared at home or enjoyed at one of the many informal restaurants found in any given neighborhood. Comfort food often involves a nostalgic element, perhaps reminding us of a childhood memory. Quite often in times of stress or challenge, we will look for relief in comfort foods. They are meals that feed the soul as much as they feed the body.

One of my favorite comfort foods is a piping hot bowl of Campbell's tomato soup (and I can indulge my craving so much more easily now that they have developed the microwavable cans). Every once in awhile, this classic American food hits the spot. Its unique sweetness and tanginess, combined with a grilled cheese, satisfies my hunger. Sitting at my kitchen table, this simple meal that originates from an everyday, ordinary container serves as a reminder of God's faithfulness and goodness. I can open my mouth and taste how good God truly is.

Just a mile or two from my home is a fairly nondescript cemetery. Most likely, I have driven by this cemetery hundreds of times and never paid a moment's notice to it. Not long ago, however, my curiosity was piqued as I learned that Andrew Warhola is buried there. On first hearing, that name may not carry much weight or significance, but there is more to the story.

Andrew Warhola was born in Pittsburgh, Pennsylvania, on August 6, 1928. He was the fourth child of Ondrej and Ulja Warhola, working-class immigrants from Mikova, a city in northeastern Slovakia, which at the time was under the rule of the Austro-Hungarian Empire. Early in his childhood, Warhola developed chorea, a disease of the nervous system that causes involuntary movements of the extremities. As a result of this illness, Warhola became a hypochondriac, developing a strong phobia of hospitals and doctors. Often bedridden as a child, he became an outcast among his schoolmates and bonded strongly with his mother. At times he was confined to bed, where he passed the time by drawing, listening to the radio, and collecting pictures of movie stars. Warhola later described this period as being very important in the development of his personality, skill-set, and preferences.

As a young adult, Warhola decided to study commercial art at what is now known as Carnegie Mellon University. After fine-tuning his artistic skills, he moved to New York City in 1949 and began a successful career in magazine illustration and advertising. During the 1950s, he gained fame for his quirky ink drawings of shoe advertisements, and around the same time, RCA Records hired Warhola to design album covers and create promotional materials for the label. In 1952, the artist had his first individual show at the Hugo Gallery, exhibiting *Fifteen Drawings Based on the Writings of Truman Capote*. Warhola's work was exhibited in several other venues during the 1950s, including his first group show at the Museum of Modern Art in 1956, and his influence in the artistic world continued to increase. And it was at this time that the artist shortened his name to Andy Warhol.

Andy Warhol became an iconic figure in American art history. By appropriating images from popular culture such as Coke bottles, one-hundred-dollar bills, and celebrity figures like Elvis and Marilyn Monroe, Warhol created many paintings that remain icons of twentieth-century art—none more important and significant than the famous Campbell's soup cans. Warhol reminded us that a soup can is more than just a soup can; there is beauty to be found in the ordinary and everyday realms of life.

While there is much in his life and worldview that was extremely warped and inconsistent with a faithful approach to biblical living, I believe Warhol tapped into the grand idea that beauty can be found in the ordinary, everyday things of life. This profound and powerful truism can inform and guide our lives, both individually and as worshipping communities of faith.

Pop artists such as Warhol brought art back into that realm of life in which everyday, ordinary people derived most of their pleasure and their experience: from television, magazines, and other media—from the things of real life. The epic, the grand, and the pretentious were replaced with the everyday; and mass-produced art was awarded the same significance as the unique and singular. The gulf between high art and low art was eroding.

There has been a great deal of discussion among art historians around the question, "what was the most significant innovation of twentieth-century art?" Some experts argue that it was the cubism movement led by artists such as Picasso, while others point to the influence of pop art. Both cubism and pop art arose from a similar place of discontentment with and rebellion against the accepted style of art. The cubists believed that post-impressionist artists were too tame and limited. Pop artists were convinced that the abstract impressionists were pretentious and over-intense, even disconnected from the rest of life, and sought to bring art back into the material realities of everyday life and popular culture, hence the term "pop."

As I was reflecting on these different reactions, a light bulb turned on inside me—might that same critique be made about worship? At times, worship can be tame and extremely limited. We try to control God. We put God in a box. We don't want things to get out of control. And yet, I must confess that sometimes worship can become more than a little bit pretentious and disconnected from real life. The reality is, we serve this incredibly glorious, magnificent Creator who cannot be tamed, constrained, or limited.

Some folks once asked me about our community of faith and our decision to rent space for our Sunday morning worship gatherings from a local elementary school rather than purchase our own facility. After my explanation, they responded, "I don't think I could worship God in a gym." Their practice of worship was connected to a particular time, space, and structure (a grand and ornate structure, I might add), and they were seemingly unable or unwilling to expand their understanding of worship beyond the walls of the cathedral or sanctuary.

Let me state this as emphatically as possible: I am a raving fan of and an advocate for pop worship. Worship needs to be real and connected to the very fabric of our common life. As we seek out and become more aware of the beautiful, the sacred, and the holy in the ordinary realms of life, our worship should then flow forth from that beauty and glorify the One who created it all. Pop worship is a way of life that encompasses the everyday, ordinary things of life.

The question I want to explore in this rest of this chapter is simple, yet extremely profound: what is worship? If we're going to spend the next one hundred pages pressing into this, it is critical to develop some common understanding and language that will help us navigate the terrain that lies ahead.

Defining Worship

Over the years I have become a collector of definitions of worship. Before digital folders existed, I kept a manila file folder close at hand, and whenever I came across some interesting thoughts or perspectives on worship, I filed them away for future reference and reflection.

Let me share some of my favorites with you. These come from a variety of people and perspectives over the ages. As you reflect upon them, keep the words of Jesus in mind: "Therefore every teacher of the law who has been instructed about the kingdom of heaven is like the owner of a house who brings out of his storeroom new treasures as well as old" (Matthew 13:52, TNIV).

As a prolific author with over thirty books to his credit, Robert Webber was and continues to be one of the most influential voices on worship in the last one hundred and fifty years. While he wrote and taught at length about worship, his understanding of the subject was grounded in his conviction that worship is celebration. According to Webber, worship is primarily "a celebration of what God has done for us in Jesus Christ."[1]

Another definition comes from Gerritt Gustafson, one of the founders of the modern worship movement. At a conference on worship leadership that I attended early in my ministry, I heard Gustafson state:

> *Worship is the act and attitude of wholeheartedly giving ourselves to God spirit, soul and body. Worship is simply the expression of our love for God, which Jesus said should involve all our heart, mind and physical strength. It's both an action and an attitude. And not just in part but holistically giving ourselves to God, our spirit, our soul, our body. It is a tangible way we express our love to God. And Jesus said it should involve our heart, our mind and our physical strength.*

When I reflect upon this understanding of worship, the word that comes to mind is the word integrity. Beyond a sense of truth telling and honesty, at its root the word integrity has this idea of completeness and wholeness. For example, an integer is a whole number (literally, a number that is "untouched"). Worship has to do with personal wholeness and the integration of our thought life, our emotional life, and our physical and relational life. As such, worship should be viewed as a whole-person activity, one that we engage with our whole being.

---

[1] Robert Webber, *Worship Old and New* (Grand Rapids: Zondervan, 1994), 28.

Years ago, I encountered an amazing thinker and artist by the name of Dieter Zander.[2] At that time, Zander was a teaching pastor at Willow Creek Community Church, where he also served as one of their worship leaders. After a season of leadership in that capacity, Zander made a radical ministry shift. Walking away from the megachurch ministry of Willow, he began a work in the San Francisco area, pioneering a movement of artists and church planters, as well as a house church movement. Zander described worship as "bringing all that we know of ourselves, in each and every moment, before all that we know of God."

As you consider Zander's definition of worship, can you see the relationship between the revelation of God and our response to that revelation? God reveals something to us about his nature, character, or attributes, and we in turn respond to God. We bring what we know of ourselves in that precise moment before what we know of God in that moment.

For example, if I find myself in a season where I come to a fresh realization of my brokenness, sin, and rebellion against God, and I am willing to bring that awareness into the presence of a God whom I know to be a God of compassion and forgiveness, I discover that God's mercies are fresh and new every

---

[2] On February 4, 2008, Dieter suffered a massive stroke that affected the left side of his brain, causing a communication disorder called aphasia. His ability to express his thoughts, plans, feelings, and faith has been severely compromised. Dieter cannot speak, write, read, or even play piano the way he used to. The creative genius that once found an outlet through words and music is now channeled through the lens of a camera. Dieter's photographs are beautiful, insightful glimpses of a new kind of hope. He calls his photos "Pictures That Talk," and you can learn more at http://www.dieterzander.com.

morning. I can revel in the reality that God is slow to anger and abounding in loving kindness, not just in theory but in real time.

During one of our Sunday morning worship gatherings, we introduced a song by Chris Tomlin and Matt Redman entitled "Our God." This popular worship song declares that God is greater and stronger than any power in the universe. As I was teaching this chorus to our community of faith, I realized afresh my powerlessness over certain attitudes and behaviors in my life. As I acknowledged what I knew of myself in that very moment, the words of the chorus became more than mere words. In the depth of my being, I began to experience the greatness, strength, and power of God being unleashed within me. And I walked away from that gathering with renewed confidence that our God is indeed awesome in power and that God's power at work in, with, and through me is my only hope in my struggle with attitudes and behaviors that do not reflect the love and grace of Jesus Christ.

One magnificent dynamic of this understanding of worship as movement is that when we respond in appropriate ways to the revelation of God (by opening our lives through humility, confession, or gratitude), God is inclined to reveal even more of himself to us. God begins to reveal different areas of our life that we have held back. As we learn more about God's nature and character, God invites us to bring more of our life into the divine light. As we grow and mature in our relationship with God, a flow and movement of worship begins to emerge—the dance of bringing all that I know of myself before all that I know of God.

Louie Giglio is the founder of the Passion movement and in that role has mentored worship leaders like Chris Tomlin, Matt Redman, David Crowder, and Christy Nockels. Giglio defines worship as follows: "Worship is our response, both personal and corporate, to God for who God is and what he has done, expressed in and by the things we say and the way we live."[3]

Worship is our response to who God is. Worship involves a personal, individual component as well as a corporate and communal response. We respond to God's initiation. We respond to God's revelation. We respond to God's character—who God is, and to God's acts in time and space—what God has done. Our worship is expressed not only by the things we say, the songs we sing, or the prayers we pray, but by the way we live.

Worship as a Diamond

One year for our wedding anniversary, I planned to surprise my wife with a beautiful diamond necklace. Now I know absolutely nothing about diamonds, other than that they are expensive and they are my wife's primary love language. Fortunately for both my wife and me, I have a friend who is in the diamond business. When I contacted Tom by phone, he invited me to visit his place of business and learn more about the major investment I was about to make.

What a learning experience that hour turned out to be. Tom patiently schooled me in the four Cs of diamonds: clarity, color, cut, and carat weight. Serious and expensive matters. But the big moment for me arrived when my friend placed a powerful tool in my hands, enabling me to examine the diamonds with greater magnification than my naked eye could possibly provide. Suddenly I was transported to a whole new realm of insight, intrigue, and discovery. Each and every diamond was unique, and as I rotated it at different angles, each gem glistened with its

---

[3] Louie Giglio, *The Air I Breathe: Worship as a Way of Life* (Colorado Springs: Multnomah Books, 2006), 53.

own particular beauty and brilliance. I continued to follow this process for some time until one particular diamond called out to me (and my budget) saying, "I'm the one." And that diamond is the one that today my wife proudly, and I might add beautifully, wears around her neck.

Worship, both our understanding as well as our practice of it, is—in a sense—like a diamond. The more you turn it and bring it into the light, the more you will see the beauty of God and the wondrous ways that God has created us to be in relationship with him, both as individuals and as communities of faith. Each facet inspires me to love God more deeply and to express my worship more passionately. However, of all the diamonds I have shared with you regarding the essence of worship, there is one that informs my understanding and practice most fully.

Alexander Schmemann was a prominent twentieth-century Orthodox Christian priest, teacher, and writer. While he possessed a deep love and appreciation for the liturgy of the historic church, what distinguished Schmemann from other Orthodox church leaders was his conviction that the liturgy of the church was never to be separated from the mission of the church in the world today. Schmemann emphasized a sacramental approach to worship but—consistent with his overall world and life view—saw no division between the sacred and secular. The church, in both its communal and individual expressions (and I would include its gathered and scattered dimensions as well), is called to a sacramental[4] life, and this includes both the sacrament of the world and the sacrament of

---

[4] While there are many different understandings of the sacraments in the church today, I am using this term to describe the tangible expressions that mediate to the people of God the mysteries of the grace and goodness of God in Jesus Christ.

the kingdom. God offers the gifts of the world to humankind, and we in turn receive them with thanksgiving and gratitude. Unlike any other part of the creation, we have the unique capacity to respond to God's blessing.

Schmemann believed that all people are intended by God to live a sacramental life and that our highest calling is to live as priests:

> *The basic definition of man is that he is priest. He stands in the center of the world and unifies it in his act of blessing God, of both receiving the world from God and offering it to God—and by filling the world with this eucharist, he transforms his life, the one that he receives from the world, into life in God, into communion with Him.*[5]

A eucharistic lifestyle is one in which a person receives the whole of life with gratitude and then in turn offers that life back to God as a source of blessing to others.

This leads me to share my definition of worship: worship is offering our lives back to God for the sake of the world.

It is critical to take the time to unpack this understanding of worship. I invite you to consider the rest of this chapter as an opportunity to explore together this definition of worship under the scope. Turn it, view it, and explore it with me from a number of different vantage points and angles. And in so doing, may your understanding as well as your practice of worship be enhanced.

The Apostle Paul, in his letter to the church in Rome, commands the first followers of Jesus to live their lives in a distinct way: "Therefore I urge you, brothers and sisters, in view

---

[5] Alexander Schmemann, *For the Life of the World: Sacraments and Orthodoxy* (Yonkers: St. Vladimir's Seminary Press, 1997), 15.

of God's mercy, to offer your bodies as a living sacrifice, holy and pleasing to God. This is true worship. Do not conform to the pattern of this world, but be transformed by the renewing of your mind. Then you will be able to test and approve what God's will is, his good, pleasing and perfect will" (Romans 12:1–2 TNIV).

Twenty-first-century followers of Jesus need to pay careful attention to these first-century instructions. Rightly understood, these words contain the power and potential to unleash a revolution of worship in the world today. Consider the revolutions that were unleashed by Guttenberg's printing press, the splitting of the atom, the invention of personal computers or the discovery of wireless technologies. How much more might a revolution of worship change our world by bringing life, restoration, and hope?

Consider the first aspect of the diamond—Paul's starting point and understanding of worship: all that we do must be in response to whom God is and what God has done for us in Jesus Christ. So before Paul says, "Become worshippers," he urges his listeners, with every ounce of passion and conviction he can muster, to consider the incredibly wondrous and gracious things God has done for them in Jesus Christ. To use an analogy from the theater, the backdrop for a life of worship must be the mercy, compassion, and love of God. To live with these qualities of God as our backdrop is to live with an ongoing experience and appreciation of the concrete expressions of God's love and grace.

Please take note that Paul is speaking to the entire church, a community of faith that consisted of both men and women, along with boys and girls. When we read, "Therefore I urge you, brothers and sisters," we are reminded that worship is not relegated to one gender or one station or season of life. The instructions given to the early church were a clear reminder that the activity and action of worship are something that all God's people are called to express and engage. It is intended by God to be an experience for the whole body of faith.

Turn the text again and see the second dimension as the call "to offer your bodies as a living sacrifice, holy and pleasing to God." The word that Paul uses for offer is *parasthsai*, which means "to place at the disposal of another." The implication here is that God is the giver of life, and as such, God grants people the freedom to live their lives as they choose. Every individual is confronted with a choice and a decision both daily and even moment by moment: will I live my life for myself or will I live for something or someone outside of self? In a sense, Paul is declaring, "In light of God's concrete expressions of love or grace, be ready and willing and quick to offer yourself back to God, to place your body at the disposal of another, the one who created you, redeemed you, and sustains you." This is a free choice: there is no coercion whatsoever on God's part. An invitation is extended, and we must choose whether we will freely give our lives back to God or offer them to some other cause or master. Bob Rognlien, in a book entitled *Experimental Worship: Encountering God with Heart, Soul, Mind and Strength*, makes an interesting observation about the relationship between freedom and worship when he writes, "There's only one thing that God does not have—our worship."[6]

Rolling Stone has described the music of American indie band Death Cab for Cutie as "melodic, melancholy songs about feeling both smart and confused, hopelessly romantic but wary of love."[7]

---

[6] Bob Rognlien, *Experiential Worship: Encountering God with Heart, Soul, Mind and Strength* (Colorado Springs: NavPress, 2005), 30.

[7] "Transatlanticism," *Rolling Stone Magazine*, November 10, 2003, http://www.rollingstone.com/music/albumreviews/transatlanticism-20031110.

Their song "I Will Possess Your Heart," was nominated for a 2009 Grammy in the category of best rock song. It features a lengthy, extended, and repetitive instrumental introduction that is anchored solidly around a particularly haunting bass groove. The tension builds over the three-minute introduction, after which singer Ben Gibbard plaintively declares that, after spending some time together, he will possess his lover's heart. The singer is determined (and I might even suggest obsessed) to possess his lover's heart. He is committed to doing everything humanly possible to ensure that one day this desire will become reality. And yet the open-endedness of the song leaves the listener pondering the final outcome.

God is not only our creator but also the lover who desires deeply to possess our hearts. But the reality is that unless and until we choose to give God our worship, it is the one thing God does not possess. Consider this reality for a moment: God has everything in the heavens above and in the earth below. The morning stars, the sun, and the moon—they all give glory to their creator. The fish in the sea and the birds of the air all give glory to their creator. But until we freely choose to offer our very selves back to God through our worship, God does not possess it.

God speaks through the prophet Isaiah:

> *Forget the former things;*
> *do not dwell on the past.*
> *See, I am doing a new thing!*
> *Now it springs up; do you not perceive it?*
> *I am making a way in the desert*
> *and streams in the wasteland.*
> *The wild animals honor me,*
> *the jackals and the owls,*
> *because I provide water in the desert*

> *and streams in the wasteland,*
>   *to give drink to my people, my chosen,*
>   *the people I formed for myself*
>   *that they may proclaim my praise. (Isaiah 43:18–21)*

The Message describes God's people in Isaiah 43:21 with these words: "the people I made especially for myself, a people custom-made to praise me." We have been custom-made by our creator to proclaim God's praise through our lives; but again, God allows us to either live into our purpose or pursue a life that reflects the shape of someone or something else.

Turn the diamond a third time. Paul declares to the Romans (and to us as well) that we are to offer our bodies as living sacrifices. I appreciate what Kenyan Bible scholar David Kasali writes about the word body:

> *Here the word "body" represents far more than just our belongings or our money. It means the totality of our life plans and activities. The offering of ourselves is a spiritual act of worship that we can give to God. Through our bodies we express what we think, what we have, and how we live. Our bodies are containers. Our bodies are vehicles. Our bodies are instruments to express what we think, what we have, and how we live and we are to offer them to God as a living sacrifice.*[8]

Isn't that quite a strange turn of a phrase—a living sacrifice? It is an oxymoron in that everyone knows what typically happens to sacrifices. They die. They are offered up, killed, and consumed. However, things are different in God's economy. Keeping in mind

---

[8] Tokunboh Adeyemo, ed., *The African Bible Commentary* (Grand Rapids: Zondervan, 2006), 1395.

the trajectory that God has set forth in Jesus, the one who gave his life, the one who died and the one who lives again, we also in that same spirit can offer our lives back to God. Dying to self and personal agendas and being willing to set aside one's own purposes is, in God's kingdom, the pathway for experiencing the full, rich, and abundant life that God has in mind for his people.

Turn this text one more time. We are not to offer our lives to anything or to anyone. We are called to offer them back to God. Why? Because God is our creator and we are the creation.

One of the podcasts in my regular listening queue is that of Rick McKinley. Rick serves as the lead pastor of a missional community of faith located in Portland, Oregon, called Imago Dei. In a podcast entitled "Breathe," McKinley said, "The starting point of worship is coming to grips with the reality that our very life and breath is a gift from God. We offer our lives back to God in full recognition that God is the source of life. We have no life and we have no breath, apart from what God gives to us."[9]

As I was listening to McKinley's teaching, for some strange reason the lyrics to Bon Jovi's rock anthem "It's My Life" came to mind. While this may be a great rock anthem, its theology does not measure up. The life that we possess does not ultimately belong to us.

In actuality, it is God's life that is graciously given to us. Imagine for a moment what it would look like if each and every day we lived with a greater awareness that life is a gift that freely comes to us from the hand of God. And in full recognition of that reality, what would it look like to willingly offer it back to God and in the service of others?

[9] Rick McKinley: Breathe, *Imago Dei Community*, September 24, 2006, http://www.imagodeicommunity.com/sunday/sermon-archive/breathe/.

Now there is one significant obstacle and roadblock in this whole worship deal. The problem is that we offer our lives imperfectly back to God. Not only is what we offer to God imperfect, but also the way we offer our lives to God is marred and distorted by the reality of our sin, brokenness, and alienation. This is actually a gigantic problem because God is a perfect God and a holy God. God is indeed worthy of the entire creation's perfect worship. And yet we, as imperfect human beings, offer imperfect gifts.

How then can we ever please God? How can our worship bring joy and pleasure and delight to our Creator? And how then can we ever hope to offer our lives back to God for the sake of others? The reality is that there is only one way that our worship can become acceptable to God. There is only one way our worship can bring delight to our God and blessing to others. It is through the offering of Jesus.

There is a book near the end of the New Testament called Hebrews that I find to be one of the deeper documents in all of Scripture. In the book of Hebrews, the writer is speaking to followers of Jesus who were deeply rooted in Jewish traditions, rituals, and practices. They had come to understand Jesus as their awaited Messiah and were now committed to following him. Captivated by the message of Jesus, along with the message of the early church, they sought to integrate the new ways of Jesus with the established ways of Judaism. However, as time progressed, these first-century followers reverted back to their default ways of thinking about and relating to God. Their past experience with God had been grounded on ritual, routine, and a sacrificial system that was dependent upon the blood of animals being offered on the temple altar in Jerusalem.

Over and over again, the writer of Hebrews tells these believers that Jesus is the fulfillment of all things. Jesus is the great high priest, far superior to any human priest who has ever offered any animal sacrifice in any temple. Because of the sacrifice of Christ and through the offering of his own life upon the cross, there is no longer a need for any person to make any sacrifice on any altar at any temple. His sacrifice is perfect, complete, and all sufficient.

The writer of Hebrews describes the offering of Christ and his priestly service this way:

> So now we have a high priest who perfectly fits our need, completely holy, uncompromised by sin, with authority extending as high as God's presence in heaven itself. Unlike the other high priests, he doesn't have to offer sacrifices for his own sins every day before he can get around to us and our sins. He's done it once and for all, offered up himself as the sacrifice. The law appoints as high priest men who are never able to get the job done right, but this intervening command of God which came later appoints the Son, who is absolutely, eternally perfect. (Hebrews 7:26–28 The Message)

Jesus has offered himself once and for all—for all people, for all time. He has offered up himself as the one holy sacrifice, and he does so in and with perfection. It is clear from the law of God that the most important and greatest commands are to love God with our whole heart, mind, soul, and strength and to love our neighbors as ourselves. Jesus loved God and others perfectly, completely, and fully.[10] Therefore, Jesus can offer his life back to God in a perfect way. This enables us to view Jesus as the perfect example of worship. More than any other human worship leader (and we all know about the cult of worship leaders), Jesus is the model for worship leadership because he is the only one who has ever made a perfect sacrifice. He is the only one who has perfectly and completely offered his life back to God for the life of the world.

In Chapter 2, I referenced the work of James Torrance and his book, *Worship, Community and the Triune God of Grace*. Torrance addresses the critical nature of Christ's priesthood and the significant role it plays in our worship: "Here is the one true priest, the one true worshipper, the leader of our worship in whom alone the ordinances of worship are perfectly fulfilled, and through whom alone we can draw near to God. So worship is God's gift of grace to us in Christ."[11]

During one of the highly-rated seasons of the TV show *American Idol*, I came across a cartoon that featured a pastor behind a pulpit along with a member of the choir who had just concluded singing a solo. Titled "Too Much American Idol for Pastor Martin," the cartoon's caption reads (think Randy Jackson or Simon Cowell), "Thank you for that solo, Jill. A little pitchy up front but then you relaxed and you really brought it home."

Our worship is by no means perfect. Our worship, both individually and communally, is more than a little bit pitchy. One of our technical guys in our community of faith records our Sunday worship gatherings and then edits them for our podcast. I

---

[10] Matthew 22 and also OT references from Deuteronomy and Leviticus. Scot McKnight's book *The Jesus Creed* provides great insight into the priority of this command in Jesus' teaching and life.

[11] Torrance, *Worship, Community and the Triune God of Grace*, 63.

have to confess it is quite the miraculous process. But even with the best editing software and technology money can buy, there is one thing that Joe cannot do—he cannot make our worship gatherings perfect. He can certainly make them better, but perfection is simply unattainable.

But there is good news: Jesus perfects our worship. God moves toward us in Jesus and graces us with love and acceptance. Through our union with Christ, we are where he is. Jesus is feasting at the table with the Father and the Spirit, and through him, we are there as well. Now that we are in Jesus, he invites us into the activity of the feast. As the ultimate worship leader, Jesus takes our song and perfects it before the Father. Jesus takes our rhythms and syncs them perfectly with the rhythms of God. Jesus takes every word, every thought, every action, every dream, and every attitude and perfects them—not because anything we offer is filled with so much potential and good, but because his sacrifice is perfect, and what we offer in faith now becomes pleasing to God.

Take your soup can and place it before God as an offering.

"So here's what I want you to do, God helping you: Take your everyday, ordinary life—your sleeping, eating, going-to-work, and walking-around life—and place it before God as an offering." That is the way Eugene Peterson translates Paul's words from Romans 12. Take your ordinary, everyday life, not some pretentious fantasy life, not some tame and limited life. Take your real life, your unique life, your one and only life—your broken, sinful, flawed life—and through Christ, offer it back to God who in turn wants to use it to bring life to others.

Perhaps Andy Warhol's biggest contribution to pop culture was his idea that everyone would possess his or her own personal "fifteen minutes of fame." This expression, "fifteen minutes of fame" is actually a paraphrase of a line in Warhol's exhibition catalog for a February/March 1968 exhibit at the Moderna Museet in Stockholm, Sweden. The catalog stated, "In the future, everyone will be world famous for fifteen minutes." Years later, Warhol reiterated this claim declaring, "My prediction from the sixties finally came true: in the future everyone will be famous for fifteen minutes."

The concept of fifteen minutes of fame is enticing, especially in a day and age when our cultural landscape is dominated by reality TV and Twitter updates. However, understanding worship as the act of offering our everyday, ordinary lives back to God for the life of the world reminds us that the highest goal in life is not realized in the seeking and securing of a fleeting moment of fame, significance, or impact, but rather in following the example of Jesus who honored God and became a life-giving agent to others. That is a vision for life that calls forth the best in and from us—people who will make a difference both in the here-and-now and throughout eternity. Eternity starts now!

four

worship and mission

Worship must include: loving our neighbor, seeking justice for the downtrodden, evangelism, and the renewal of true community.
—*Alan Hirsch*

Mission exists because worship does not.
—*John Piper*

For we are to God the pleasing aroma of Christ among those who are being saved and those who are perishing. To the one we are an aroma that brings death; to the other, an aroma that brings life. And who is equal to such a task?
—*2 Corinthians 2:14-16*

One of the most potent aromas in the universe is coffee. While coffee is a massive global industry, I am a relative latecomer to the game, as I did not experience my first cup until my mid-thirties. My entry into the caffeinated world was hardcore—black, no cream or sugar. And there has been no turning back, as I spend a portion of almost every working day in one of my favorite local coffee shops, partaking of large amounts of coffee as rich and bold as possible.

As a small child, I remember shopping with my father in the old A&P grocery store near our home. One particular aisle always captured my interest, the aisle with the self-serve coffee grinder. People would scoop up their beans, fill the grinder, and flip the switch. The sound was actually frightening to a young child, but the smell that followed was so amazingly intoxicating that it was worth the momentary scare.

Imagine my delight when years later, I found myself in a mountainous region of central Ethiopia, the birthplace of coffee, where I experienced an authentic Ethiopian coffee roasting ceremony. Right before my eyes, two Ethiopian woman, dressed in their tribal clothing, began roasting the beans, filling the room with an incredible aroma. After the beans were roasted to perfection, the women ground them and prepared the finest, most flavorful cup of coffee I have ever had the privilege of partaking. This beautiful ritual, along with beans that contained both velvety notes of dark chocolate and subtle hints of sweet citrus produced a cup of coffee that was simply amazing!

Coffee is such a rich, sensual experience, so I find it strange that in most coffee shops, a lid is placed on your cup immediately after it is poured! Our sense of taste is deeply connected to our sense of smell, and it is critical in how we experience the taste of something to have the ability to smell it.

We have a wonderful, rich cup of coffee that smells fantastic and we put a lid on it. Why? Convenience? Of course. To keep it hot longer? Absolutely. But the primary reason is safety. Remember the warning on the cup: "Caution—the beverage you're about to enjoy is extremely hot." In reality, we put lids on our coffee to make it safer. We are willing to sacrifice the richness of the experience for safety.

Coffee helps me think more expansively about worship. When our understanding and practice of worship is confined to the safety of our sanctuaries, it reminds me of a freshly brewed cup of coffee with a lid tightly fastened. Just as the aroma of coffee should not be constrained to a cup, our worship was designed to move beyond the confines of buildings and be released into the world. What might happen if God's people took a few more risks and started living more dangerously? What would it look like if we let the aroma of our worship begin to move out of our sanctuaries and into the world? What if our lives began to boldly manifest the goodness of our God?

The Dangerous Act of Worship

We live in a culture that is captivated by extreme things. People are looking for ways to push the envelope, live on the edge, and obtain the coveted adrenaline rush. For example, consider the rise of extreme sports and events like the X Games. These activities require a degree of skill and ability, and any poor execution during the activity can result in serious physical harm to the participant. In other words, there is a significant level of danger and risk involved.

When is the last time you thought of worship as a dangerous activity? Mark Labberton introduced me to that idea in his book *The Dangerous Act of Worship*. He writes:

> *When worship is our response to the One who alone is worthy of it—Jesus Christ—then our lives are on their way to being turned inside out. Every dimension of self-centered living becomes endangered as we come to share God's self-giving heart. Worship exposes our cultural*

and even spiritual complacency toward a world of suffering and injustice. In Jesus Christ, we are called into a new kind of living. Through the grace of worship, God applies the necessary antidote to what we assume is merely human—our selfishness. Worship sets us free from ourselves to be free for God and God's purposes in the world. The dangerous act of worshiping God in Jesus Christ necessarily draws us into the heart of God and sends us out to embody it, especially toward the poor, the forgotten and the oppressed. All of this is what matters most and is most at stake in worship.[1]

Labberton states that the dangerous act of worship draws us into the heart of God. However, this phrase "the heart of God" is a loaded one. Countless times over the course of my ministry, people have said to me, "I want to go deeper into the heart of God." More often than not what they are seeking is a more personal experience with God. They are looking for those intimate moments of communion and oneness, or to use Old Testament temple language, they seek to move from the outer courts into the Holy of Holies.

In the beloved *Chronicles of Narnia*, C. S. Lewis tells the story of four children who walk through an old wardrobe and are magically whisked away to the mystical land of Narnia. Inside Narnia they discover a snowy land, talking animals, an evil White Witch, and a powerful lion named Aslan.

It is not necessary to be an expert in Christian theology to recognize the imagery Lewis injects throughout this work. There is a fascinating dialogue that takes place early in the story, shortly

---

[1] Mark Labberton, *The Dangerous Act of Worship: Living God's Call to Justice* (Downers Grove: InterVarsity Press, 2007), 14.

after the four children come to Narnia. Upon meeting a talking beaver, they agree to accompany him back to his house where they enjoy a lovely dinner Mrs. Beaver has prepared. When the meal is finished, Mr. Beaver tells the children that he is going to take them to see Aslan. Lucy, the youngest of the four, asks if Aslan is a man.

> *"Aslan a man!" said Mr. Beaver sternly. "Certainly not. I tell you he is the King of the wood and the son of the great Emperor-beyond-the-Sea. Don't you know who is the King of Beasts? Aslan is a lion—the Lion, the great Lion."*
>
> *"Ooh!" said Susan, "I'd thought he was a man. Is he— quite safe? I shall feel rather nervous about meeting a lion."*
>
> *"That you will, dearie, and no mistake," said Mrs. Beaver; "if there's anyone who can appear before Aslan without their knees knocking, they're either braver than most or else just silly."*
>
> *"Then he isn't safe?" said Lucy.*
>
> *"Safe?" said Mr. Beaver; "don't you hear what Mrs. Beaver tells you? Who said anything about safe? 'Course he isn't safe. But he's good. He's the King, I tell you."[2]*

Worship that draws us into the heart of God is not for the timid or faint of heart. It is dangerous and risky and will move us out of our comfort zones and take us to places we have never imagined.

---

[2] C. S. Lewis, *The Lion, The Witch and the Wardrobe* (New York: HarperOne, 1978), 48.

A Consecrated Life

If worship is offering our lives back to God for the life of the world, this demands that we place our lives at the disposal of another, namely God.

Frances Ridley Havergal (1836–1879) was the daughter of a church rector raised in nineteenth-century England. Possessing a love for learning, she became an astute student of the Scriptures, even becoming proficient in both Hebrew and Greek. She was also a gifted singer and pianist. However, her heart's desire was to have a lasting spiritual influence upon others. Havergal discovered that she could do this through her writing, and for that reason, she expended the majority of her life's labors in writing both prose and poetry that would be spiritually beneficial to God's people. Although Havergal suffered poor health and died at the age of forty-two, her work had significant impact, not only in her own day, but for future generations as well.

Havergal's most well-known work is the hymn "Take My Life:"

Take my life and let it be
Consecrated, Lord, to Thee.
Take my moments and my days,
Let them flow in endless praise.

Take my hands and let them move
At the impulse of Thy love.
Take my feet and let them be
Swift and beautiful for Thee.

Take my voice and let me sing,
Always, only for my King.
Take my lips and let them be
Filled with messages from Thee.

Take my silver and my gold,
Not a mite would I withhold.
Take my intellect and use
Every pow'r as Thou shalt choose.

Take my will and make it Thine,
It shall be no longer mine.
Take my heart, it is Thine own,
It shall be Thy royal throne.

Take my love, my Lord, I pour
At Thy feet its treasure store.
Take myself and I will be
Ever, only, all for Thee.

She described the circumstances behind the writing of this hymn:

> *Perhaps you will be interested to know the origin of the consecration hymn, 'Take My Life.' I went for a little visit of five days. There were ten persons in the house, some unconverted and long prayed for, some converted but not rejoicing Christians. He gave me the prayer, 'Lord, give me all in this house!' And He just did! Before I left the house everyone had got a blessing. The last night of my visit I was too happy to sleep, and passed most of the night in praise and renewal of my own consecration, and these little couplets formed themselves and chimed in my heart one after another, till they finished with, 'Ever, only all for Thee!'*[3]

---

[3] Louis Benson, *Studies of Familiar Hymns* (Philadelphia: Kosta Press: 1903), 213.

When Havergal declared, "Take my life and let it be, consecrated Lord to thee," she was willingly offering the totality of her life to God. Her consecration was first to Christ, but always in service to others. Havergal rightly understood that worship calls us to offer and consecrate our lives with the recognition that God is the one who not only creates us but also redeems and gifts us for God's purposes in the world.

The Heartbeat of God

A number of years ago, during a routine visit, my primary care physician spent a little more time than I was comfortable with listening to my heart. After removing the stethoscope from his ears, he said to me, "I do not like what I am hearing; we need to run some additional tests." With those words, I was welcomed into the world of EKGs and echocardiograms.

My most recent echocardiogram showed some potentially serious issues and so I sought out a second opinion with one of the finest cardiologists in the city. Working out of a university research medical setting provided this physician with state-of-the-art technology that enabled him to take a good look at the condition of my heart. After a thorough study of all my tests, I heard the words every cardiac patient longs to hear, "Your heart looks really good. You are going to die of something someday, but it most likely will not be heart-related."

If God were willing to submit to cardiac testing, what would we find?

It is rare that I reference the King James version, but I have been intrigued by how this translation captures an experience of Jesus and one of his disciples. In the closing days of his life on earth, Jesus gathered his followers together in an upper room and as they reclined around the table together, John's gospel records these words: "Now there was leaning on Jesus' bosom one of his disciples, whom Jesus loved" (John 13:23, KJV).

"Jesus' bosom"—don't you love the sound of those words? Imagine if you had the opportunity to rest your head on the bosom of Jesus. What would you hear? Of course it would be sound of the steady heartbeat of the Son of God, each beat pulsating with divine love. It is interesting to note that the beloved disciple leaning on the bosom of Jesus was also the author of the fourth gospel, the only gospel which records these words: "For God so loved the world that he gave his one and only Son, that whoever believes in him shall not perish but have eternal life. For God did not send his Son into the world to condemn the world, but to save the world through him" (John 3:16–17).

While God welcomes us and invites us to find in divine love a place of refuge and comfort, God's heart is for the world and is always extending and reaching out. Those who rightly discern the heartbeat of God will not be content to remain leaning on Jesus' bosom, but will be motivated to move out from that place of love into the world that God so loves.

Bob Pierce, the founder of World Vision, prayed, "Break my heart, O God, with the things that break your heart."

What breaks God's heart?

The Missio Dei

God is for the world. God loves the world and this divine love moves God into action. God has a plan for the world that encompasses the redemption of all things. Theologians have coined the phrase *missio dei* to describe not only God's heart, but also God's plan to restore and renew everything. Think for a moment about God in missionary terms. God is a sending God who sends Jesus into the world that God passionately loves. This missionary paradigm is captured brilliantly in John 3:16–17 which speaks of both God's love for the world and God's intention to save the world.

Missiologist Stuart Murray describes the missio dei as follows:

> *God is the Missionary, who sent His Son and sends His Spirit into the world and whose missionary purposes are cosmic in scope, concerned with the restoration of all things, the establishment of shalom, the renewal of creation, and the coming of the kingdom of God, as well as the redemption of fallen humanity and the building of the Church.*[4]

Murray's description of God's mission being "cosmic in scope" is a potent phrase, encompassing every dimension of creation and culminating in the rescue of a people who because of sin have been alienated from their creator. This rescue plan also includes the formation of a community for whom God would be their deepest source of joy. Jesus called this community the church; and while Jesus truly wants his people to find in the church a comforting presence, it was never his intention that his followers would be content to sing songs, pray prayers, and listen to well-prepared and compelling sermons. While our life in Christ certainly includes the experience of corporate worship, the deeper life of worship that God has in mind for God's people includes our participation in God's mission in the world.

Near the end of John's gospel, we find a lengthy prayer that Jesus offered just prior to his arrest in the Garden of Gethsemane. Jesus prays that he would bring God glory by finishing the work

---

[4] Stuart Murray, *Church Planting: Laying Foundations* (Scotdale: Herald Press, 2001), 39.

that he was sent to do, the work of offering his life for the life of the world. But Jesus prays not only for himself, he prays as well for his disciples, for those who would follow in his footsteps. "As you have sent me into the world, I have sent them into the world. For them I sanctify myself, that they too may be fully sanctified" (John 17:18–19).

These words are missional in nature, implying that God's intention for the church is much more than gathering together in beautiful cathedrals or multiple purpose gymnasiums for times of worship. "As the Father has sent me, so I send you" reflects God's heart for the world, God's plan to rescue all things, and God's intention to use redeemed people in the process.

As the early church took shape and form, the Apostle Paul stated the critical role that the church plays in the redemptive purposes of God: "His intent was that now, through the church, the manifold wisdom of God should be made known to the rulers and authorities in the heavenly realms, according to his eternal purpose that he accomplished in Christ Jesus our Lord" (Ephesians 3:10–11). In other words, there is no Plan B. God's redemptive purposes in the world are actualized by forgiven people, living by the power of the Spirit, participating in the missio dei.

The heartbeat of God is love and this love is at work in the world today, restoring the broken and dislocated parts of the universe, atom by atom, piece by piece, putting them back together again. It all happens because of Christ's death, his blood poured down from the cross. As God's people, we have the privilege, honor, and responsibility to proclaim this reality in word and deed. God has a mission, and the church is a missional community partnering with God wherever and whenever we are able in the life-giving process of seeing the world renewed in Jesus Christ.

The key to living missionally is worship. A person will only be able to reflect the love of God to the world if that person is worshipping the one true God, the one who has created the world from an overflowing, self-giving love. The more a person enters into the heart of God and celebrates that love, the more that person will be able to reflect that overflowing, self-giving love as they move into the world.

This is why engaging in corporate worship is so important. One of the things that can happen when the church gathers for worship is that the people come into contact with the powerful love of God in Jesus Christ. In a sense, God shines the divine light of love on the gathered ones. When this occurs, the gathered can experience an intimate encounter with God; however, this encounter is not an end in itself. God extends light and love upon the church in order that the church might go into the world and shine, becoming reflectors of God's love. But the people of God will not be able to engage in mission effectively unless they take seriously the call to corporate worship, living deeply together in the love of God, revealed most powerfully in the giving of God's own Son Jesus.

Jesus is the ultimate worship leader. There is good reason that the Scriptures call us to "fix our eyes upon Jesus, the author and finisher of our faith." Because Jesus perfectly offered his life back to God, as we offer our worship to God through his, our worship is perfected as well. This is good news to those who are prone to sing off key, pray less than grammatically correct prayers, or lose attention while listening to a sermon. Though our acts of worship may be less than perfect, through Christ they become not only acceptable to God, but pleasing as well.

Jesus, as our model worship leader, not only offers his life to God, but also offers it for the life of the world. In John 6, Jesus miraculously feeds the multitudes with the five loaves of bread and two fish that a young child willingly offered to Jesus. While the crowd found satisfaction in the meal that was provided, the people became confused between the physical things that Jesus offered and the spiritual realities that Jesus was presenting. The physical bread satisfied them for a few hours, but Jesus was offering something that could fulfill their deepest needs. As he taught the people, Jesus declared, "I am the living bread that came down from heaven. Whoever eats of this bread will live forever. This bread is my flesh, which I will give for the life of the world" (John 6:51). In speaking of his death on the cross, Jesus was proclaiming that his sacrifice was more than that of a martyr. His was a generative offering, bringing real life to the world.

You might look at all the activity that occurs in the world—the creativity, the innovation, the opportunity and possibility—and ask, "is not the world already alive?" Yes and no. While the world is in one sense alive, at the very same time, it is filled with death. The results of sin are all around us: war, terror, relational brokenness, sickness and disease, corruption, injustice. This world is under a death sentence and Jesus offers his very life in order that the world might come back to life.

This is the missio dei. As Jesus offered his life back to God for the life of the world, we can participate in the work of restoration and renewal by offering our lives, through Christ, back to God for the life of the world.

Taking Off the Lid

But thanks be to God, who always leads us as captives in Christ's triumphal procession and uses us to spread the

69

aroma of the knowledge of him everywhere. For we are to God the pleasing aroma of Christ among those who are being saved and those who are perishing. To the one we are an aroma that brings death; to the other, an aroma that brings life. And who is equal to such a task? (2 Corinthians 2:14–16)

In writing these words to the church in Corinth, Paul was recalling an event that those living in the Roman empire would be quite familiar with, the triumphal procession. Awarded by the senate to honor a victorious military hero, this was an enormous parade that occurred in the heart of Rome. The festivities might last several days and the entire population of Rome would line the streets to view the spectacle. The capital city would be festooned to embrace her conquering hero, with incense rising up from every temple. Often the pageantry would include the plunder taken from the enemy, especially captured soldiers. The captives would be led before the chariot of the conquering general, and subjected to the mockery and taunts of the onlookers. The climax of the procession involved a sacrifice to the Roman deities and the execution of any captives in the forum. In his *Jewish Wars*, the historian Josephus described the triumphal procession, "It is impossible to describe the multitude of the shows as they deserve, and the magnificence of them all."

Why in the world would Paul use this image? What did this picture of the triumphal procession mean to Paul, and how did he envision himself as a player in the festivities? The larger context of the text reveals that rather than seeing himself as a victorious soldier, Paul places himself in the scene as the conquered subject. At first glance this is shocking—because conquered enemies were put to death at the end of the processional as a sacrifice to the

Roman gods. But Paul understood himself as God's captive being led to death. As Scott Hafemann writes:

> *Paul's metaphor in 2:14 may be "decoded" as follows: As the enemy of God's people, God had conquered Paul at his conversion call on the road to Damascus and was now leading him, as a "slave of Christ" (his favorite term for himself as an apostle), to death in Christ, in order that Paul might display or reveal the majesty, power, and glory of God, his conqueror.[5]*

In other words, Paul, seeing himself as the conquered one, was offering his life back to God for the life of the world. Kent Hughes explains it this way:

> *As faithful followers of Christ, Paul and the apostles were the sweet aroma of Christ rising up to God, irrespective of the human response to their message. As they preached, the smoke of Christ's sacrifice ascended to God, well-pleasing to him. Thus, the primary audience in Heaven was glorified. But the aroma also had a horizontal and mutually exclusive effect upon the people who heard—"to one a fragrance from death to death, to the other a fragrance from life to life" (v. 16a). The smell of incense would have had different connotations to the victors and to the captives in the procession—namely, life and death. The apostolic witness would be "a fragrance from life to life" for those who believed and "a fragrance from death to death" for those who rejected it.[6]*

---

[5] Scott Hafemann, "Profiles of Expository Preaching." *Southern Baptist Journal of Theology.* Summer 1999.

[6] R. Kent Hughes, *2 Corinthians: Power in Weakness (Preaching the Word)* (Wheaton: Crossway Books, 2006), 38.

What kind of aroma spills forth from our lives? Is it a fragrant one that is life-giving and causes others to flourish and thrive? What happens when we take the lid off?

One of the members of our community of faith works as the director of alumni relations at a local university. Heidi is one of the finest young leaders I know, possessing a strong work ethic, incredible people skills, and a deep commitment to let her faith inform her work. The university where she serves helps students connect their faith, learning, and serving, believing that through these connections they can become agents of transformation in their communities and the world.

As part of her responsibilities at the university, Heidi has had the opportunity to participate in numerous service-learning trips, taking small groups of students and alumni into the developing world. She has made a dozen visits to the Centro Nutricional y Hogar de Ninos (Nutritional Center and Children's Home) in Patzun, Guatemala, and her heart as been captured by the children who call this place home. She returns year after year because she desperately wants to make the lives of these children better, in ways large and small. During each trip, the students engage in a physical project such as building a school or constructing a health clinic. Each of these projects brings real help and hope in tangible ways. But the heart of her visits is the time she spends with the children. Heidi and the students bring a ministry of presence, playing games, singing songs, and simply but powerfully loving on these little ones. Heidi has chosen to take the lid off her life and allow the love, mercy, and compassion of Jesus Christ inside her spill over into the lives of a small collection of the children who God so loves. In so doing, Heidi is participating in the missio dei, joining with God in the work of renewing and restoring all things.

A few years ago my friend Glenn, husband and father to two teenage daughters, was diagnosed with throat cancer. He is the poster boy for the adage "what doesn't kill you makes you stronger." Glenn was determined to beat this terrible disease, and his pathway to healing involved an aggressive plan that included heavy doses of chemotherapy and radiation treatments. In the midst of his treatment, I will never forget leaving the hospital and thinking to myself, this man is so close to death; if the cancer does not kill him, the treatment certainly will. Yet he refused to give up or give in. Convinced that God was not yet finished with him, he battled on and, today, is cancer free.

While some are content to celebrate the reality that they are survivors, Glenn chose to remove the lid from his life. Buoyed by his journey toward healing, Glenn is constantly looking for opportunities to share, in word and deed, the message of hope. Whether it is writing his personal story for a newsletter or website, visiting someone recently diagnosed, or speaking to a support group, this much is clear: Glenn's passion is to be a voice of hope. Joining in the missio dei, the aroma of Glenn's life is rich and thick with hope.

Some time ago, I received a letter that reminded me of the importance of taking the lid off our life, even in small and seemingly insignificant ways. As the return address on the envelope was unfamiliar, I was leery of opening it, fearful that it might be some kind of anonymous critique of my preaching or leadership. Facing my fears however, I opened the letter and discovered these words:

> *Dear Terry, You know the saying "action speaks louder than words"? Well, it's very true, and true when it comes to you. You were a huge encouragement to me whether you realize it or not.*

While I was in high school I had a really tough time. My parents and my relationship were not the best. I was struggling with physical abuse from them. My sophomore year, one of my closest friends invited me to attend her youth group. I went and after a few weeks of attending I accepted Christ as my Savior. I was broken. And I felt the hurt and pain that grew inside of my heart. And I felt like it was healing. I went away for college and it was the best decision for me. I was on my own, out of the house, etc.

After I graduated from college I took a job at a newspaper here in Pittsburgh. Half of the reason I took the job at Panera was because the adjustment to Pittsburgh was a lot harder than I expected. I found myself down and depressed many days. During the harder times in high school I was really depressed and struggled with depression and suicidal thoughts. I even attempted once. I did not want that to happen all over again when I felt that way when I moved to Pittsburgh. And so working in Panera helping others and seeing the same people day after day and having those friendly conversations kept me going.

But also every day I could see you reading or helping someone. And that encouraged me. You. Your actions were a blessing. I can remember one day sitting in Panera probably slicing bread or something and you were talking to a man with a child. You talked for a while. And the man just started crying. You comforted him. And I thought to myself, wow, now that's God working. In short I want to thank you. Thank you for the effect that you had on me that you will never fully understand. You were a blessing and an encouragement beyond words.

The man she was referring to was Carlos, a friend of mine whose forty-year-old wife had recently died after a long and brutal battle with brain cancer. Ginny's death created a huge void in his life and the lives of their three daughters, and I met regularly with him throughout her illness and after her death, trying my best to create a safe space for my friend to process his emotions. Never once did I imagine that we were being watched.

Have you ever stopped to think that perhaps you are being watched as well? You probably give it no second thought as you go about the business of your life. But the truth is there are broken, hurting people all around us, people who have been caught up in patterns that result in sadness, pain, and death in all its forms. As we take our everyday, ordinary lives and offer them back to God, we have the privilege to partner with God in the work of renewal and the opportunity to see some of the dislocated and broken pieces of the universe be restored in Christ.

In an interview with *Christianity Today*, N. T. Wright said, "The key to mission is always worship. You can only be reflecting the love of God into the world if you are worshiping the true God who creates the world out of overflowing self-giving love. The more you look at that God and celebrate that love, the more you have to be reflecting that overflowing self-giving love into the world."[7] Wright reminds me that worship is not only connected to mission, but that mission is also linked to worship. As we offer our lives in worship, we participate in God's great mission. And

---

[7] N.T. Wright, "Mere Mission," *Christianity Today,* January 5, 2007, http://www.christianitytoday.com/ct/2007/january/22.38.html.

as God's mission unfolds and bears fruit in this world, others will join the ranks of worshippers as well.

What would it look like if you took the lid off your life? Imagine what might happen if you stopped playing it safe, forgoing convenience and comfort to take up a risky and dangerous life of worship? How can you begin to let the aroma of your life in Christ rise up in the places where you live, learn, work, serve, and play? May it be the fragrance of life to the world God so loves.

worship as work

The Christian life is marked by the offering of one's self to God to be shaped, empowered, directed and changed by God. In worship, God presents us with the costly self-offering of Jesus Christ. We are claimed by Christ and set free. In response to God's love in Jesus Christ, we offer God our lives, our gifts, our abilities, and our material goods, for God's service.

—The Book of Common Worship

You say grace before meals. All right. But I say grace before the concert and the opera, and grace before the play and pantomime, and grace before I open a book, and grace before sketching, painting, swimming, fencing, boxing, walking, playing, dancing and grace before I dip the pen in the ink.

—G. K. Chesterton

When my wife Patty and I first began participating in the life of the local church, a typical lunch conversation would start with this question, "Was it educational or inspirational?" We would then proceed to dissect the worship service, most particularly the sermon, and force it into one of our two categories. As young Christ followers, we were convinced that the primary purpose of corporate worship was either educational or inspirational in nature. After a few months of this conversation, we noticed that we were being pinged back and forth in worship, one week engaging our minds, plumbing the depths of the deep truths from Scripture and the next Sunday having our emotions touched, being moved and motivated to live more faithfully and passionately for Jesus.

What if worship is more than education or inspiration?

Recently, author Donald Miller created quite a firestorm in the blogosphere with a post entitled, "I Don't Worship God by Singing. I Connect With Him Elsewhere." With an honesty not often seen in Christian circles, Miller wrote:

> *It's just that I don't experience that intimacy in a traditional worship service. In fact, I can count on one hand the number of sermons I actually remember. So to be brutally honest, I don't learn much about God hearing a sermon and I don't connect with him by singing songs to him. So, like most men, a traditional church service can be somewhat long and difficult to get through.*

> *I'm fine with this, though. I've studied psychology and education reform long enough to know a traditional lecture isn't for everybody. There's an entire demographic of people who have to learn by doing, not by hearing. So you can lecture to them all day and they're simply not going to get it.*

> *Research suggest (sic) there are three learning styles: auditory (hearing), visual (seeing) and kinesthetic*

(doing) and I'm a kinesthetic learner. Of course churches have all kinds of ways for you to engage God including many kinesthetic opportunities including mission trips and so forth, but if you want to attend a "service" every Sunday, you best be an auditory learner. There's not much out there for kinesthetic or visual learners.[1]

Donald Miller is a strong and passionate follower of Jesus. I have absolutely no reason to doubt the sincerity of his faith commitment and his desire to grow in his relationship with Christ. He wants to connect with God, and yet his experience of corporate worship has been less than fulfilling. I think part of Miller's problem is that he is equating worship with either education (learning about God) or inspiration (being moved emotionally through music). In a follow-up post, Miller outlined nine reasons why he does not attend church with regularity. His concluding thought was that the church is not willing to adapt beyond a lecture/worship system. He writes:

I do think church can evolve beyond a lecture / worship / performance institution, but the current leadership is unlikely to make that happen. When and if the church evolves, it will evolve from outside the current leadership and that evolution will pose a threat to existing tribal values as well as financial systems that are sustained by the current model. In other words, the church will be reluctant to change because things that are foreign are perceived as bad and we've got to keep doing it this way for job security...

---

[1] Donald Miller, "I Don't Worship God by Singing," *Storyline Blog,* February 3, 2014, http://storylineblog.com/2014/02/03/i-dont-worship-god-by-singing-i-connect-with-him-elsewhere/.

Neither am I arguing the current model should change.
Millions are fed weekly through these kinds of programs.
What I'm arguing is that nobody should be faulted for
creating something different. Those who would argue
"we shouldn't simply create the church in our own
image" forget it already has been created in our own
image. First the image of the royal government then the
image of the university or school and then big business
and now moving toward the entertainment industry.
The church has always been recreated in the image of
the dominant institution in society. For the early church,
that was the family. For our culture, it's business and
education and entertainment.[2]

Miller is not alone in his experience. My guess is that his words reflect the experience of countless Christ followers in the United States and other Western nations. I appreciate his willingness to wade into these waters, as it opens the doors for dialogue about the true purpose of worship. And I think that Miller's framework of worship as education and entertainment is at the heart of the problem.

Education, Entertainment, or Experience?

Years ago, I attended a conference at a megachurch in Southern California. Part of the experience included an opportunity to participate in a question and answer session with the senior pastor. As a student of worship, I was particularly intrigued when someone asked the pastor to describe what constitutes a good worship service. Without hesitation he replied,

---

[2] Donald Miller, "Why I Don't Go to Church Very Often," *Storyline Blog,*
February 5, 2014, http://storylineblog.com/2014/02/05/why-i-dont-go-to
-church-very-often-a-follow-up-blog/.

"A good worship service is when I preach a biblically sound, sixty-minute sermon."

Welcome to the world of worship as education.

Have you noticed that many of the larger churches in the United States have strong, charismatic communicators? These faith communities are built on a foundation of teaching, and the centerpiece of their weekly gatherings is the proclamation of the Word. Historically, the church has a long legacy of instructing the people of God, and, according to the book of Acts, the first followers of Jesus devoted themselves to the apostles' teaching (Acts 2:42). Since the earliest days of the church, various segments of the body of Christ have expressed their commitment to the preeminence of teaching. Some faith communities are no longer calling their worship spaces sanctuaries, but rather auditoriums—a word derived from the Latin meaning "pertaining to hearing." The design of the space, with seats facing forward, provide some not-so-subtle hints to the priority of the service. It could be argued that today's church may be perhaps the most well-taught church in history; but while there is certainly a pedagogical component to worship, the focal point of biblical worship is not the sermon.

If teaching is not the focus of corporate worship, what is? Once again, church architecture may provide some clues. Many churches have moved beyond the auditorium and are now designing their worship space around the concept of the theater. The goal has become to maximize the audiovisual aspect of the service. In these contexts, a music leader might have more power and influence in a local church than a teaching pastor. Think about it. Churches place their musicians on a platform (church-speak for stage), invest significant amounts of financial resources on audiovisual technology, and then devote twenty to forty minutes of the service to music. In the best-case scenarios, musicians understand that they are performing for an audience of One; in less optimum contexts, the musical performance becomes a mini-concert, with the musicians onstage entertaining the gathered congregation.

As a trained musician and someone who leverages his musical background on a regular basis, I place great value on the role that music plays in creating worshipful environments. Unfortunately, in some cases musical leaders have been elevated to superstar status.

"If we are not rock stars, what are we?" This is the question that Stephen Miller raises in his book *Worship Leaders: We Are Not Rock Stars*. He writes:

> *A worship leader is to be a person who exemplifies worship in all areas of life as an example for the church to emulate; who pursues God with everything and lives a life of holiness that worships through obedience in all things; who leads the church in an all-encompassing lifestyle of worship. Part of the disconnect that has led to the prominence of rock star worship syndrome in the church is that people have failed to understand this all-of-life nature of worship.*

> *They want to compartmentalize worship to the seventy-five minutes on Sunday morning. If Sunday morning songs are the church's only worship experience all week, there is no wonder that we have placed such a hard emphasis on having the best, most musically gifted song leader. But such a focus on music and the music leader is*

often at the detriment to the myriad other aspects of worship, both personal and corporate.[3]

Music has historically played a vital part in the worship life of the church. Yet it seems that the modern church has gone a long way from Paul's instructions to the church in Colossae to "let the message of Christ dwell among you richly as you teach and admonish one another with all wisdom through psalms, hymns and songs from the Spirit, singing to God with gratitude in your hearts" (Colossians 3:16).

While there is an educational component to worship as well as a strong desire to captivate people's attention through musical expression, there is a third and equally powerful factor that impacts the contemporary corporate worship gathering: experience. We live in an experience economy, a phrase coined by Joseph Pine and James Gilmore and later expounded on in their book *The Experience Economy: Work as Theatre and Every Business a Stage*. Pine and Gilmore suggest that the entire history of economic progress can be summarized in the four-stage evolution of the birthday cake:

As a vestige of the agrarian economy, mothers made birthday cakes from scratch, mixing farm commodities (flour, sugar, butter, and eggs) that together cost mere dimes. As the goods-based industrial economy advanced, moms paid a dollar or two to Betty Crocker for premixed ingredients. Later, when the service economy took hold, busy parents ordered cakes from the bakery or grocery store, which, at $10 or $15, cost ten times as much as the packaged ingredients. Now, in the time-starved 1990s,

---

[3] Stephen Miller, *Worship Leaders, We Are Not Rock Stars* (New York: Moody Publishers, 2013), Kindle edition, location 255–262.

parents neither make the birthday cake nor even throw the party. Instead, they spend $100 or more to "outsource" the entire event to Chuck E. Cheese's, the Discovery Zone, the Mining Company, or some other business that stages a memorable event for the kids— and often throws in the cake for free. Welcome to the emerging experience economy.[4]

The experience economy has influenced the way worship takes place in the local church.

Places of worship are now offering color-coordinated themes that provide a coffeehouse look, feel, and smell. Children and youth are invited into adventure-themed environments where they can experience firsthand the truth of the Scriptures. At one level, this is an encouraging and necessary development: God has created people with senses to be engaged and emotions to be touched. As a designer of worship experiences in the local church, I lobby strongly for the creation of multi-sensory gatherings where people can taste and see how good God is. Yet my deep concern is that we may end up seeking the experience of worship rather than experiencing a life-changing encounter with the God who is worthy of worship.

The Hipster Conservative blog, in response to Donald Miller's post about church attendance, raises some worthwhile considerations. If the purpose of corporate worship is *learning about Jesus*, you might have a better learning experience by reading a book, listening to a podcast, or streaming a video. Your pastor is most likely not a Hebrew or Greek scholar but rather a

---

[4] B. Joseph Pine II and James Gilmore, "Welcome to the Experience Economy," *The Harvard Business Review*, July 1998, http://hbr.org/1998/07/welcome-to -the-experience-economy/.

person of slightly above average intelligence trying to balance his or her teaching responsibility with a myriad of other ministry functions. Let's be honest: not every Sunday morning message is going to be as informative and inspiring as the latest TED talk.

If the purpose of corporate worship is *entertainment*, perhaps you should consider going to a movie theater, art gallery, or musical concert. They will do a better job than most local churches.

If the purpose of corporate worship is to *experience God emotionally,* the Sunday gathering may not deliver the goods. We may very well not experience God emotionally at any church gathering.[5]

What if worship is more than education, more than entertainment, more than experience? What if worship was seen as work?

Worship as the Work of the People

This idea of viewing worship as work is not a new approach. Actually the church has thought about worship as work for many generations. In fact, one of the primary words the church has used to describe worship has at its heart the concept of work. That word is liturgy, an idea derived from the Greek *leitourgia,* meaning "the work of the people." Originally this word was used to describe the public responsibilities of citizens, and it was eventually co-opted by the church, which began using it to describe the formal rites and practices of corporate worship. Alexander Schmemann, building upon this understanding of

---

[5] *The Hipster Conservative* (blog), February 4, 2014,
http://hipsterconservative.com/2014/02/04/donald-miller-doesnt-need-to-go
-to-church/.

worship as the work of the people, describes liturgy as "an action by which a group of people become something corporately which they had not been as a mere collection of individuals—a whole greater than the sum of its parts."[6]

Today liturgy is understood as the work that God's people do together whenever they gather. Think about the variety of forms and expressions liturgy may take: sitting, standing, kneeling, reading, singing, genuflecting, affirming, declaring, greeting, giving, listening, and blessing. It may include formal written prayers, responsive readings, and classic hymns from past generations; or liturgy may take the form of Spirit-led intercession or spontaneous singing.

Some people may be familiar and conversant with liturgy because of their background in the Catholic or Anglican tradition. But many today describe their current church experience as non-liturgical. Honestly, there is no such thing as a non-liturgical church. All churches have a pattern, flow, and rhythm to what they do when they gather. Have you ever noticed that even churches that claim to be "Spirit-led" typically have the same structure from week to week and service to service? I have found that the important question is not, "Am I liturgical?" but rather, "Is my liturgy good?"

There is a Latin phrase—*lex orandi, lex credendi, lex vivendi*—that is translated "as we worship, so we believe, so we live." This reminds me that liturgy shapes us. The prayers we pray, the songs we sing, the activities and actions of worship—they form us in conscious and subconscious ways. James K. A. Smith makes this point quite forcefully when he speaks of human beings as "homo liturgicus." Liturgy occurs both inside the walls of the church

---

[6] Schmemann, *For the Life of the World*, 25.

during corporate worship and outside the walls of the church in our everyday, ordinary lives. You don't believe me? When is the last time you went to your local shopping mall or sports or concert venue? We are a liturgical people, and these institutions, with their well-designed routines, rituals, and rhythms, communicate important values and shape the way we view not only the world, but also ourselves.

In my part of the world, there is a ritual that occurs almost every weekend during the months of September through December. The Pittsburgh Steelers are one of the most successful professional sports franchises in the world, and their accomplishments on the field strongly influence our regional psyche. Throughout the fall season, the people in my city take great pride in donning their black and gold and bearing the colors of the "Steeler nation" in our schools, the workplace, and yes, even in our sanctuaries. This tribe of passionate fans extends beyond our city as a network of Steeler bars and establishments have cropped up around the country, creating spaces for the faithful to gather and cheer their beloved team to victory. The Steelers possess six championship trophies, the most of any team in the National Football League. Whenever the trophies are publically displayed, the fans flock to gaze at this "holy grail" of football. The Steeler nation is a liturgical people, and our rituals and shared practices inform not only the way we view ourselves, but also the world around us, thus shaping our common life. For "as we worship, so we believe, so we live."

Avodah

Allow me to introduce you to one of my favorite Hebrew words, *avodah*. This potent word, used over two hundred times in the Old Testament, provides a pathway to an integrated life.

What I find fascinating about the word is that it is employed in three different ways. In some places avodah is translated as "work," in other places as "serve," and at other times as "worship."

The first reference comes from the creation narrative in Genesis. The Lord God plants a beautiful garden and fills it with all sorts of pleasing things, including the tree of life and the tree of the knowledge of good and evil. In Genesis 2:15 we read, "the Lord God took the man and put him in the Garden of Eden to work [avodah] it and take care of it." God takes the first man and assigns him a meaningful purpose—to care for and steward the creation. The creation was good, but it was incomplete. Pregnant with possibility, God called Adam and Eve to the work of bringing out creation's potential. This has become known as the cultural mandate, the charge from God to all of humanity to not only enjoy the creation, but to work it as well.

Work is a gift from God. This may be news to you. For years, I believed that work was the unfortunate result of the fall, an unintended consequence to humanity's disobedience. If Adam and Eve had simply followed God's commands, I would not be laboring over the writing of these words (or any other tasks that are part of my daily work). But a careful reading of the creation narrative reveals that work (avodah) has a central place in God's original intentions for humanity. Tim Keller defines work as "rearranging the raw materials of a particular domain for the flourishing of everyone."[7] His words remind me that to be human is to be a worker, charged by God to take the goodness of the creation and to make much of it, to the end that the common good is served and that others flourish and prosper.

---

[7] Tim Keller, *Every Good Endeavor: Connecting Your Work to God's Work* (Dutton, New York: 2012), 59.

Now it is true that the narrative of the fall, found in Genesis 3, illustrates a change in how we experience work. As the result of sin, work now becomes labor. We all realize this on a daily basis, whether it be in the frustrations of the marketplace, difficulties in the work of parenting, or the struggles of being a student. But we should never forget that God's original purposes for work (avodah) were good.

Another way that avodah is used is to describe our service, both to others and to God. This word carries the sense of a person submitting themselves to the purposes of another, whether it be a servant to a master, a son to his father, or a subject to a king. In Deuteronomy we read, "And now, Israel, what does the Lord your God ask of you but to fear the Lord your God, to walk in obedience to him, to love him, to serve [avodah] the Lord your God with all your heart and with all your soul" (Deuteronomy 10:12).

Currently, I serve on the board of directors for two non-profit organizations, both of them engaged in the work of leadership development, one locally and the other in the East African nation of Uganda. Because I believe so strongly in the catalytic role that leaders play in organizational life, I have made the decision to align my purposes and expend my resources of time, energy, and money to serve the larger purposes of the organization. This service involves work—committee meetings, conference calls, and strategic planning sessions. These organizations promote the common good and are committed to God's purposes in the world today, and my connection with them enables me to offer my work in service to both God and others.

The third way avodah is used is to describe worship, whether it is worship of idols or worship of the one true God. When God calls Moses to lead the Hebrews out of Egypt, God gives Moses this promise: "When you have brought the people out of Egypt, you will worship [avodah] God on this mountain" (Exodus 3:12). And in Exodus 8:1, the Lord said to Moses, "Go to Pharaoh and say to him, 'This is what the Lord says: Let my people go, so that they may worship [avodah] me.'"

Unfortunately, for many in our culture, work has become an idol. The drive to succeed is powerful and many have bowed the knee to this idol that promises much more than it can actually deliver. We need a framework that helps us think correctly about the integration of work, service, and worship. For me, the biblical concept of avodah has provided a framework for understanding that my work is a means by which I can both worship God and serve my neighbors. While we can worship through our work, we must not worship our work. Avodah is the pathway to getting this right.

Living Liturgically

Each day presents a fresh opportunity to integrate our work, our service, and our worship. As we open our eyes, climb out of our beds, and engage the world around us, God is extending an invitation to live liturgically, to participate in the work of God. And this invitation calls for a response.

To help heighten this reality in our faith community, we have been using the language of RSVP. We have been challenging people to accept God's invitation to make all things as they should be in the places we live, learn, work, serve, and play. As part of this focus, we have been collecting the stories of people who are doing exactly that in a series we call "Everyday Faith."

I think Eugene Peterson brilliantly captures this call and response with his translation of the words of the Apostle Paul to the church in Rome: "So here's what I want you to do, God helping you: Take your everyday, ordinary life—your sleeping, eating, going-to-work, and walking-around life—and place it before God as an offering" (Romans 12:1, *The Message*).

This is the epitome of living liturgically, not only on Sundays, but the other six days of the week as well. In this text, Paul is drawing on the language of worship as he calls the people of God to offer their everyday, ordinary lives to God. Paul's initial audience would have been well-versed in a sacrificial system of worship, be it the Jewish temple system or pagan systems. Whether the offering was made to fulfill the mandate of the Jewish law or to appease an angry god, in either case that which was offered was sacrificed.

The NIV translates Paul's words here as "offer your bodies as a living sacrifice, holy and pleasing to God—which is your spiritual service of worship."

Bruce Benson, in his book *Liturgy As a Way of Life*, uses the framework of "intensive liturgy" and "extensive liturgy" to describe the interplay between the worship that occurs on Sunday and the worship that takes place throughout the other six days.

> Intensive liturgy is "what happens when Christians assemble to worship God." Within intensive liturgy, we meet the living Christ by way of Word and sacrament. Through intensive liturgy, we are taught, sustained, and fed. On the other hand, extensive liturgy is "what happens when Christians leave the assembly to conduct their daily affairs." We are sustained and fed precisely in order to go out into the world. Of course, these two kinds of liturgy are wholly dependent upon one another. It is not as if we could have one without the other. "As our intensive liturgies drive us into the world to do our

extensive liturgies, so our extensive liturgies bring us back week by week to the Christian assembly.[8]

God is inviting us to join in the amazing work of making all things as they should be in the places we live, learn, work, serve and play.

Making the World a More Beautiful Place

Each week I spend a significant amount of time and energy creating our Sunday morning worship gathering. My deep desire is to craft a beautiful liturgy, to do everything I can to shape an environment that points worshippers toward the good, the beautiful, and the true, and enables them to taste and see how good God is. Creating good liturgy is a work of art. And as important as that is on Sunday mornings, it is equally as important throughout the other six days of the week. "For we are God's handiwork, created in Christ Jesus to do good works, which God prepared in advance for us to do" (Ephesians 2:10).

Not long ago I had the opportunity to participate in a daylong seminar on servant leadership in the marketplace, featuring a number of nationally and internationally known speakers on the subject. Each presentation provided both fresh information and much-needed inspiration to live more faithfully in the marketplace, bearing witness to the goodness of God through the exercise of leadership modeled upon the principles embodied by Jesus Christ.

The highlight of the day for me occurred when leadership guru extraordinaire, Ken Blanchard, interviewed a close friend of

[8] Bruce Ellis Benson, *Liturgy as a Way of Life: Embodying the Arts in Christian Worship* (Grand Rapids: Baker Publishing Group, 2013) Kindle edition, Location 1983–1988.

mine about his practice of servant leadership in the marketplace. My friend spoke of his long-term investment as a leader in the creation of a company with an ethos built upon the values of servanthood and love. These values differentiate his company from others in its sector, shaping not only the way his company conducts their everyday business but also how these values contribute to the creation of a healthy bottom line.

My friend's perspective of his Monday through Friday activity and service to the company was much more than secular work, much more than simply occupying time or creating wealth until he could get on with the truly important work of ministry and building for the kingdom. Instead, he understood the marketplace as the appropriate venue to live out his calling and exercise his gifts as a leader, honoring God with the work of both his head and his hands.

This interview was a strong reminder that all over the world, men and women of faith are offering up their work daily as their act of worship to God and service to others, building organizations that are not only profitable, but also contribute to the creation of shalom in our world. Knowing that my friend's story was representative of a larger movement occurring in the marketplace helped me taste and see the goodness of God.

Brittney is a dance major at a local university, and as a follower of Jesus, she is thinking deeply about the intersection between her work as a student and her worship. Not long ago we interviewed Brittney for an "Everyday Faith" story, and I loved her response to the question, "How does dance fit into God's plan to redeem the world?"

I believe there will be a whole bunch of dancing and celebrating in heaven, and I think He gives us this gift of dance now so we can have a taste of what it will be like in heaven. I also believe dance can teach and enlighten others in ways that some would never expect. Dance can be a means of healing from the brokenness of the world, not only mentally but physically as well. Dance relieves stress and worry, and it allows me to release the tension from this world and let God handle it from there. While I'm dancing, I'm able to "let go and let God."

Dance has helped me accept God's invitation into my daily life because dance is what I do every day. I go to school and dance, I go home and dance in my apartment, and I do it pretty much every waking moment. I love it and see it as a way for me to be in conversation with the Lord, whether it be worship, thanksgiving, prayers of needs, or just a time to release my worries. I see God there—in my dancing and in others. Dance has been a reminder of the glory of God in my everyday life. Every day I remember it is the gift I have been granted, and that I need to cherish it and live the life the Lord has called me to live.

In his book *The Artisan Soul*, Erwin McManus writes,

Though we may create many beautiful works of art, the most important works of art to which we will ever give ourselves are the lives we live. No matter what else we produce in life whether we are painters or filmmakers or dancers or poets, even if you create something that might someday be kept in the gallery or museum somewhere in the world for generations of people to come and marvel at the wonder of our work will never create anything more powerful or significant than our lives. The complexity is that we are both works of art and artists at work.[9]

Consider your work. Are you a parent or grandparent? A student? Are you employed in the arts, education, or the business sector? What would it look like to place your work before God as an offering?*

Today, look for opportunities to say yes to God's invitation to make all things as they should be. Today, offer your work in the marketplace, the neighborhood, and the school as an act of worship. In so doing, may you make our world a more beautiful place, a place where others can taste and see how good God is.

[9] Erwin McManus, *The Artisan Soul* (New York: HarperOne, 2014), 12–13.
* For practical ideas, see the *Everyday, Ordinary Liturgy* included at the end of this book.

worship in a fractured world

Integrity is the courage to meet the demands of reality.
—Henry Cloud

Confront the most brutal facts of your current reality, whatever
they might be. AND, at the same time retain faith that you will
prevail in the end, regardless of difficulties.
—Jim Collins

T rue confession: I am fascinated with personality assessments. In fact, I have never met a personality test I did not like. Over the years, the Myers-Briggs Type Indicator has revealed me to be an ISTJ, the Enneagram a Number 3 (the Achiever), and the DISC assessment documented that my unique behavioral style leans toward dominance and influence. Growing in self-awareness is key to both emotional and spiritual maturity, and I am convinced that self-awareness is intimately connected to an increased awareness of God.[1]

While I highly commend to you the pursuit of more intensive work in the area of personality, for the purposes of this chapter, I invite you to take a moment and work through a quick assessment. Are you an optimist or a pessimist? Are you a glass-half-empty or half-full kind of person? Do you view the world through rose-colored glasses or lenses with a distinctly dark tint?

Although I am a big fan of optimism, I have noticed a disturbing trend in some circles of Christianity where optimism, under the guise of faith, becomes distorted to the nth degree. These followers of Jesus are creating a "Christian bubble," and when faced with the harsh realities of life, at best they ignore—and at worst, they gloss over—the painful experiences of life. This kind of person goes through life like a horse wearing blinders, unable (or unwilling) to see what is actually happening in the world. Instead, they operate with an unrealistic attitude that could be summarized with the phrase, "It's all good."

Perhaps you have witnessed this worldview. Or maybe in the midst of a difficult season of life, you have unfortunately been on the receiving end of statements such as these:

> *There is a silver lining in every cloud*
> *God needed another angel*
> *At least you can get pregnant again*
> *It will all work for good*
> *It just wasn't meant to be*
> *You have to realize that life goes on*

---

[1] John Calvin began his *Institutes of Christian Religion* with these words: "Our wisdom, insofar as it ought to be deemed true and solid wisdom, consists almost entirely in two parts: the knowledge of God and of ourselves."

This attitude is embarrassing and exasperating, and at times, approaches heresy. An "it's all good" mentality is a distortion of both the historic teaching and practice of the Judeo-Christian faith tradition. A vibrant faith was never intended to be experienced as a whitewashing that sanitizes the world of trouble, trial, hardship, and outright evil. Rather, faith is a posture that empowers people to confront the brutal realities of life and yet never give up hope. This is paradoxical in nature, and I realize that worshipping God as the sovereign, all-powerful One while living as a realist is no easy task. However, if we are going to extend our worship beyond the safety of the sanctuary and into the real world, it is a paradox we must confront.

Facing Reality

The goal of this chapter is simple: face reality. Things are not the way they ought to be. All is not right with the world. There are things that are wrong—absolutely, positively wrong. The reality is that we live in the midst of a broken, fractured world.

In chapter one, I shared the story of my nephew's marriage ceremony, a personal experience of inexplicable brokenness. My brother-in-law's absence at his son's wedding reminded me of the stark reality that things are not as God intended them to be. In your own life, how do you experience the brokenness of the world? Take a moment and conduct a quick scan of the headlines. What kinds of things do you notice? How would you characterize the stories?

What is wrong with this world? There is warfare around the globe, nation warring against nation, and civil strife pitting tribe against tribe and people group against people group. We live in a constant state of elevated terror, a world in which suicide bombers blow up train stations and public gathering spaces like marathon racecourses, inciting fear and taking innocent lives. I am writing these words on the day that the state of Connecticut released its chilling report on the Sandy Hook shooting, a horrific act of violence that resulted in the deaths of twenty first-grade students and six adults.

What is wrong with the world? The brokenness is evident, near and far and everywhere in between. Disease. Death. Poverty. Injustice. Alienation. We experience brokenness in our own relationships. The divorce rate continues to escalate, and the incidence of addiction, depression, and mental illness are skyrocketing. Perhaps there are painful realities that have come to light in your own relational circles over the past hours or days.

Clearly, things are not the way God intended them to be. The hard, cold truth is that we live in a fractured world. And yet, we are called to feast.

The Practice of Lament

Fortunately, as modern people, we have a deep well of tradition from past generations from which we can draw. This ancient wisdom can guide us as we seek to make sense of our contemporary world. Within the Old Testament, there is a collection of poems and prayers known as the Psalms. Each of the one hundred and fifty psalms conveys a unique perspective and vantage point, and the different authors give voice to a wide range of emotional experiences. There are psalms of thanksgiving and intercession, psalms of praise and deliverance, and psalms of confession. But perhaps the particular genre of literature from the Old Testament that can best inform and instruct our feasting in a fractured world is that of lament.

Laments dominate the landscape of the Psalms. (Laments are also found throughout the Old Testament prophets, and there is

even an entire book devoted to this genre called Lamentations.)
There are both personal laments and corporate laments. Speaking
of laments, D. A. Carson writes, "There is no attempt in Scripture
to whitewash the anguish of God's people when they undergo
suffering. They argue with God, they complain to God, they weep
before God. Theirs is not a faith that leads to dry-eyed stoicism,
but to a faith so robust it wrestles with God."[2]

Let's delve deeper into one particular lament found in Psalm
44:

> *We have heard it with our ears, O God;*
> *our ancestors have told us*
> *what you did in their days,*
> *in days long ago.*
> *With your hand you drove out the nations*
> *and planted our ancestors;*
> *you crushed the peoples*
> *and made our ancestors flourish.*
> *It was not by their sword that they won the land,*
> *nor did their arm bring them victory;*
> *it was your right hand, your arm,*
> *and the light of your face, for you loved them.*
> *You are my King and my God,*
> *who decrees victories for Jacob.*
> *Through you we push back our enemies;*
> *through your name we trample our foes.*
> *I put no trust in my bow,*
> *my sword does not bring me victory;*
> *but you give us victory over our enemies,*
> *you put our adversaries to shame.*

---

[2] D. A. Carson, *How Long O Lord? Reflections on Suffering and Evil* (Grand
Rapids: Baker Academic, 2006), 67.

> *In God we make our boast all day long,*
> *and we will praise your name forever. Selah (vv. 1–8)*

Inserted into the text at the end of verse 8 is the Hebrew word *Selah*. While scholars debate its exact meaning, most believe it is a prompt to pause, reflect, ponder, and consider what has been declared. It is strategically placed in the midst of this psalm.

The psalmist begins by reflecting upon the past and proclaiming, "We have heard. We have heard of your greatness, God. We have heard the stories of how you had been at work in the community of faith, how you rescued, how you delivered, how you planted, how you sustained. How you brought about victory for God's people. Because we have heard of your greatness, your power, and your might, we declare that you are king and God. And in you, O God, we make our boast all day long. And we will praise your name forever."

This is a good place to be and calls forth celebration. However, immediately after this "Selah" moment, there is a significant change in the emotional tenor of the psalm. The writer employs a poetic technique to press the point home. While the English language often uses rhyme to create a poetic flow, the Hebrew approach was different. One of the methods the Hebrews employed was a poetic device known as parallelism, in which the first line of the poem would declare something, followed up by a second line that would state the same idea in a different way. Instead of a poetic rhyming scheme, the Hebrews used a poetic conceptual scheme. Watch how this unfolds in the following verses:

> *But now you have rejected and humbled us;*
> *you no longer go out with our armies.*
> *You made us retreat before the enemy,*

and our adversaries have plundered us.
You gave us up to be devoured like sheep
and have scattered us among the nations.
You sold your people for a pittance,
gaining nothing from their sale.
You have made us a reproach to our neighbors,
the scorn and derision of those around us.
You have made us a byword among the nations;
the peoples shake their heads at us.
I live in disgrace all day long,
and my face is covered with shame
at the taunts of those who reproach and revile me,
because of the enemy, who is bent on revenge. (vv. 9–16)

The Israelites saw themselves as a rejected people, retreating before their enemies, being devoured like sheep, and sold for a pittance. They were a reproach to their neighbors and living in disgrace because of an enemy hell-bent on revenge. This was their reality. And they actually believed that God had something to do with their situation.

All this came upon us,
though we had not forgotten you;
we had not been false to your covenant.
Our hearts had not turned back;
our feet had not strayed from your path.
But you crushed us and made us a haunt for jackals;
you covered us over with deep darkness.
If we had forgotten the name of our God
or spread out our hands to a foreign god,
would not God have discovered it,
since he knows the secrets of the heart?

Yet for your sake we face death all day long;
we are considered as sheep to be slaughtered. (vv. 17–22)

This is lament at its finest. Can you sense the desperation? "Where are you, God? What in the world are you doing?" This is more than a sense of being abandoned by God; there is a clear sense of God's hand being against them. "You know all things, God. We have faithfully followed your covenant; we have not forgotten your holy name or raised our hands to foreign idols, and yet we face death all day long. We are sheep about to be slaughtered. God, where are you?" This is a dark season for the people of God.

Walter Brueggeman in *The Message of the Psalms: A Theological Commentary* writes,

> *The use of these "psalms of darkness" may be judged by the world to be acts of unfaith and failure, but for the trusting community, their use is an act of bold faith, albeit a transformed faith. It is an act of bold faith on the one hand, because it insists that the world must be experienced as it really is and not in some pretended way. On the other hand, it is bold because it insists that all such experiences of disorder are a proper subject for discourse with God. There is nothing out of bounds, nothing precluded or inappropriate. Everything properly belongs in this conversation of the heart. To withhold parts of life from that conversation is in fact to withhold part of life from the sovereignty of God. Thus these psalms make the important connection: everything must be brought to speech, and everything brought to speech*

must be addressed to God, who is the final reference for all of life.[3]

Psalm 44 concludes with these words:

Awake, Lord! Why do you sleep?
Rouse yourself! Do not reject us forever.
Why do you hide your face
and forget our misery and oppression?
We are brought down to the dust;
our bodies cling to the ground.
Rise up and help us;
rescue us because of your unfailing love. (vv. 23–26)

Can you hear the psalmist crying out to God? "Wake up, Lord! Rouse yourself! Quit snoozing, God! Get on the job! Stop hiding your face. Bring us back to the front of your memory, O God, because we are in the dust. We are groveling, and we are barely holding on to life. Rise up and help us. Redeem us because of your unfailing love."

Henry Cloud defines integrity as the "courage to meet the demands of reality."[4] This is not a twenty-first-century concept, but one that has been fleshed out in the lives of faithful people throughout the generations. In the midst of pain, suffering, and brokenness, the psalmist maintains faith and with hope addresses God, confident that God will indeed redeem his people—not because of who he is or who the Hebrews are—but simply because of who God is, a God of unfailing love.

---

[3] Walter Brueggeman, *The Message of the Psalms: A Theological Commentary* (Minneapolis: Fortress Press, 1985), 52.

[4] Henry Cloud, *Integrity: The Courage to Face the Demands of Reality* (New York: HarperCollins, 2006), Kindle edition, location 88.

The Power of Hope

I am a relative latecomer to the whole U2 movement, having paid little attention to them (or really any other music) during the eighties. But I now have a level of obsession with this band, not simply because they are a great rock-and-roll band and not because the lead singer Bono is a hipster activist. My fascination has to do with their artistry. They are brilliant poets and prophets, artists and preachers.

I was awakened to their brilliance during a season of deep wrestling with God. It was a painful time on my spiritual journey as things were imploding around me both externally and internally. Questioning both the nature and character of God, I wondered if God was truly powerful, strong, and loving. Little did I know at the time, but I was using the language of lament.

Somehow during this season, a booklet containing the book of Psalms found its way into my hands. My curiosity about this small publication was immediately piqued as I discovered that the introduction to this piece was written by none other than Bono. The moment is still clear in my mind, holding that booklet in my hands and seeing how Bono compared reading the Psalms to singing the blues:

> *At age 12, I was a fan of David, he felt familiar ... like a pop star could feel familiar. The words of the psalms were as poetic as they were religious and he was a star. A dramatic character, because before David could fulfill the prophecy and become the king of Israel, he had to take quite a beating. He was forced into exile and ended up in a cave in some no-name border town facing the collapse of his ego and abandonment by God. But this is where the soap opera got interesting; this is where David was said to have composed his first psalm—a blues.*

*That's what a lot of the psalms feel like to me, the blues.
Man shouting at God—"My God, my God, why hast
thou forsaken me? Why art thou so far from helping
me?"*[5]

Those words triggered something deep within me, and in that moment, something transpired within me that moved my spiritual journey onto a completely different trajectory. In a sense, my faith was transformed from a simplistic, "all is right in the world" (even when it is not) point of view to a more mature, dare I say, more biblical expression, which rather than denying the reality of doubt and despair, brings them to God with the language of lament. Doubt and despair are not the antithesis of faith, but in reality, they become the pathway to a more fully orbed expression of faith.

Have you ever heard the expression, "art imitates life?" At the end of the twentieth century, U2 released an album entitled "Pop," a project that sought to musically capture the excess of the twentieth century and the self-indulgence spirit that had captivated Western culture. "Pop" begins with this incredible song called "Discotheque," a driving, pulsating song that speaks of life as one big party, celebrating the excess and the indulgence of life. And yet, as you move through the album, the tone becomes progressively darker. The album comes to a stark and somber conclusion with the last track, "Wake Up Dead Man." In retrospect, it was the last song that U2 recorded in the twentieth century, and they brought both the album and the millennium to a close with a song that cries out to Jesus, admitting to being alone in a "fucked-up" world.

---

[5] *The Book of Psalms: (Pocket Canons)* (Edinburgh: Canongate Books Ltd, 1999), introduction by Bono.

Can you hear the language of lament? "Awake, Lord! Why do you sleep? Rouse yourself! Get up and act! O my God! Where are you?"

After "Pop," U2 moved into a two-and-a-half-year period of musical silence, embracing the darkness, living in the contradiction. And then they record the album that launches them into the twenty-first century, the new millennium. The very first track on that CD is entitled "Beautiful Day," a joyful anthem that celebrates the gift of each new day. The song calls listeners to seize every moment, experience it to its fullness, and rejoice.

This music presents to me a strong call to live more faithfully in the tension between what is and what could be. How do we live in the midst of the contradictions? What does it mean to live in the darkness and the starkness of Psalm 44? To cry out, "Wake up! Where are you, God, in this midst of this fractured world?" What would it look like to live in the reality that it is also a beautiful day that God has created?

Oh God, redeem us with your unfailing love. Whether we live in the fifth century BC or the twenty-first century AD, we are called to embrace the contradictions, to live in the midst of the brokenness and yet never give up hope. As Walter Brueggemann writes, "The laments are refusals to settle for the way things are. They are acts of relentless hope that believes no situation falls outside of Yahweh's capacity for transformation."[6]

What Is Right with the World?

For years, I have worn a white wristband that simply says "One." I received this from the ONE organization, a campaigning

---

[6] Walter Brueggeman, *Old Testament Theology: Essays on Structure, Theme and Text* (Minneapolis: Augsburg Fortress, 1992), 29.

and advocacy network committed to ending extreme poverty and preventable disease, particularly on the continent of Africa. The wristband is a constant reminder of the more than one billion people who live in extreme, life-threatening poverty, and it serves as a constant reminder that all is not well in the world. While I live with plenty, more than a billion people across this planet are simply trying to survive another day. All is not right with the world. The world is not the way it should be.

Years ago, I participated in a worship arts conference at Willow Creek Church in Chicago. Upon registration, each person was given a black wristband with the question, "What's right with the world?" imprinted on it. The conference leaders encouraged participants to keep our eyes wide open throughout the event—to look for and pay particular attention to the good, true, and beautiful things we discovered over the course of our two days together.

On the campus of the church, the conference coordinators created a special place called the Hakarat Hatov room, separate from the other activities of the event. This Hebrew phrase *hakarat hatov* was unfamiliar to me; however, I soon learned that this is an expression of gratitude, with the literal translation being "recognizing the good." Throughout the event we were invited to take our discoveries into this sacred space and prayerfully give thanks to the One who is the giver of every good gift (James 1:17).

While both the invitation and this space were beautiful gifts from the event organizers, I found myself wrestling with the contradictions of living in the midst of the tensions of this world. My sensitivities to both the beautiful and the broken were heightened, and I found myself experiencing a deeper awareness that even though things are fractured and broken, as the "One" band on my wrist constantly reminds me, there is much that is good and right about God's world.

Too often in my life, I find myself asking the question, "What's wrong with the world?" as my personality tends to focus on the problems that need to be fixed. That conference provided the prompt that I needed. While living in a constant state of hakarat hatov may seem unattainable, what would it look like to take small steps toward greater gratefulness? "Recognizing the good" does not deny the painful realities of life, but instead moves faithfully into the space of contradiction and says "yes" to the good, true, and beautiful things that are all around us.

What's right with your world? Not long ago, on a glorious October afternoon, I gathered with a company of people on the deck of a beautiful country club, where I had the privilege of performing the wedding ceremony for two friends, Donna and Marc. Both of them have traveled difficult paths in life and have faced significant loss, sadness and grief. Years ago I walked with Donna and her children as her husband Dave was diagnosed with a brain tumor. In a short period of time, this vibrant, healthy husband and father succumbed to this terrible disease. Marc experienced a painful divorce and suffered a great deal of emotional and relational pain related to that failure.

For a number of years, both Donna and Marc lived alone, wondering if they would ever again experience the joy and companionship that marriage can bring. After a season of renewing an old friendship, they discovered that life together was better than life apart, and they made the decision to enter into the covenant of marriage.

Honored to officiate their service, I recognized the sacredness of the moment. In the presence of God, they pledged their love and commitment to one another, and with a profound awareness of the grief of past days, I could not help but say, "God, this is good! This is what is right with the world. These two people are celebrating the gift of love."

What's right with your world? Each Sunday morning as I provide worship leadership for our community of faith, I pay particular attention to two of our younger worshippers, Emma and Brady. They look and act like everyday, ordinary children because they are. But I am also privileged to know the backstory of their lives as both Emma and Brady were born prematurely, each of them coming into the world weeks early and weighing less than two pounds. But through the gift of medical technology, skilled physicians, and other medical professionals, Emma and Brady are thriving today. Yes, I realize that every day in the developing world, over 18,000 children die from curable and treatable diseases (and through partnerships with organizations like World Vision and Compassion International, I work to create a world in which this is not so). But on Sundays when I see Emma and Brady involved in our gatherings, I recognize the good and celebrate what God has done and is doing in their lives.

What's right with your world? What would the practice of hakarat hatov look like in your life? How could you grow in your capacity to recognize the good? If we are going to become people who are able to feast in a fractured world, we need to embrace the reality that God has a mission in this world—a mission of redemption and restoration. Here is how Eugene Peterson captures the words of the Apostle Paul as he described God's mission to make things right in the world through Christ:

All the broken and dislocated pieces of the universe— people and things, animals and atoms—get properly fixed and fit together in vibrant harmonies, all because

of his death, his blood that poured down from the cross.
(Colossians 1:20, The Message)

What's right about our world? Do you have eyes to see that moment by moment, day by day, season by season, God is renewing the world?

In the closing session of the Willow Creek arts conference, in the beauty of the sanctuary, Nancy Beach led thousands of pastors, musicians, and artists in making a number of personal declarations. The one that sticks in my mind most was this: "I will not give in to cynicism." What a powerful statement. Try saying that one aloud. "I will not give in to cynicism." Does that declaration reflect your current attitude or perhaps what your attitude might become in the days to come?

In his book *Good to Great*, Jim Collins outlines the Stockdale Principle. Collins coined this concept based on his study of the life of Admiral James Stockdale. During the Vietnam War, Stockdale was the highest-ranking United States military officer held as a prisoner of war in the infamous "Hanoi Hilton." Throughout his eight-year imprisonment, Stockdale was tortured over twenty times and endured extreme hardship.

Collins recalls a significant conversation he had with Stockdale:

> *"I never lost faith in the end of the story," he said, when I asked him. "I never doubted not only that I would get out, but also that I would prevail in the end and turn the experience into the defining event of my life, which, in retrospect, I would not trade."*
>
> *I didn't say anything for many minutes, and we continued the slow walk toward the faculty club, Stockdale limping and arc-swinging his stiff leg that had*

never fully recovered from repeated torture. Finally, after about a hundred meters of silence, I asked, "Who didn't make it out?"

"Oh, that's easy," he said. "The optimists."

"The optimists? I don't understand," I said, now completely confused, given what he'd said a hundred meters earlier.

"The optimists. Oh, they were the ones who said, 'We're going to be out by Christmas.' And Christmas would come, and Christmas would go. Then they'd say, 'We're going to be out by Easter.' And Easter would come, and Easter would go. And then Thanksgiving, and then it would be Christmas again. And they died of a broken heart."

Another long pause, and more walking. Then he turned to me and said, "This is a very important lesson. You must never confuse faith that you will prevail in the end—which you can never afford to lose—with the discipline to confront the most brutal facts of your current reality, whatever they might be."[7]

This principle brings to mind the language of lament. As people of faith, we can face the brutal facts of our current reality while still maintaining hope because God is a God of unfailing love. Once convinced of that truth, you can acknowledge the painful realities, live in the midst of the contradictions, and yet

---

[7] James Collins, *Good to Great: Why Some Companies Make the Leap and Others Don't* (New York: Harper Business, 2001), 85.

never surrender to cynicism. This is my declaration: "I will not give in to cynicism."

The final moments of the arts conference were musical in nature. We closed our days together by singing the hymn, "This Is My Father's World." While I have fond memories of this hymn from the church of my childhood, I had not sung it in many years. I quickly was reminded of the beautiful stanzas in this hymn. But in the midst of the contradictions of life, if we are going to feast in this fractured world, we need to take these words to heart:

> *This is my Father's world.*
> *O let me ne'er forget*
> *That though the wrong seems oft so strong,*
> *God is the ruler yet.*
> *This is my Father's world,*
> *The battle is not done;*
> *Jesus Who died shall be satisfied,*
> *And earth and Heav'n be one.*[8]

We feast while others go hungry. We rejoice while others grieve. We have plenty while others are lacking. Have you lived in that tension? The wrong seems oft so strong. It is all around us, yet God is the ruler. God is the king. Day by day, season by season, moment by moment, life by life—through Christ, God is putting the world back together again.

That is what is right about our world.

---

[8] Maltbie D. Babcock, "This is My Father's World," 1901.

seven

worship and justice

And what does the Lord require of you? To act justly and to love mercy and to walk humbly with your God.

—*Micah 6:8*

How many times have you raised the question, "What is required of me?" Think back to your experience in the world of education. As you walked into a classroom to begin a new semester, these thoughts were probably foremost in your mind: "What is required of me in this course?" What must I do to successfully navigate the class?"

Or consider the time you spend in the workplace, where your job description clearly outlines the responsibilities and outcomes by which you will be measured, evaluated, and compensated. What does your supervisor, human resource department, and company require of you?

This mindset can even creep into our relationships. Recently I was speaking with a Ugandan friend who was preparing for his upcoming wedding. Knowing that I have been married for many years, he peppered me with questions. "What is the secret to a good marriage? How can I become the husband my wife needs me to be?" In other words, he was asking what is required to have a successful marriage.

It is easy to become caught up in a checklist mentality, always wondering what is required to obtain the grade, master the job, or secure the relationship. The religious sphere of life is not immune to this line of thinking. For countless generations, people of faith have been asking this question: "What does the Lord require of us?"

The Life and Times of Micah

The prophet Micah (whose name means "who is like the Lord?") lived in the eighth century BC in a small town called Moresheth, about twenty miles southwest of the center of worship in Jerusalem. Micah's job description was straightforward: speak to the people of Israel on God's behalf. The problem was that both the national leaders and the common people were steeped in sin and rebellion against God. Despite opposition from the people and the many vocational hardships he faced, Micah firmly set his hope in the Lord: "But as for me, I watch in hope for the Lord, I wait for God my Savior; my God will hear me" (Micah 7:7).

Micah was concerned about the corruption that was prevalent in Israel, and he continually addressed the disconnection between the worship that was taking place in the temple and the behaviors and practices of the people in their everyday, ordinary lives. From Micah's vantage point, the corruption, hypocrisy, and injustice found in Israel's daily life were directly connected to the people's lack of understanding as to what God truly required of them as a worshipping community.

With that background in mind, consider these words:

With what shall I come before the Lord
and bow down before the exalted God?
Shall I come before him with burnt offerings,
with calves a year old?
Will the Lord be pleased with thousands of rams,
with ten thousand rivers of olive oil?
Shall I offer my firstborn for my transgression,
the fruit of my body for the sin of my soul?
He has shown you, O mortal, what is good.
And what does the Lord require of you?
To act justly and to love mercy
and to walk humbly with your God. (Micah 6:6–8)

In Micah's day, worship was anchored around the sacrificial system, and worshippers would approach God with something in their hands. It might be a calf, ram, or other animal that would be placed on the altar to be consumed by holy fire before God. In other cases, worshippers might bring vats of olive oil, pouring it out as an offering to the Lord. Some among the people of God even asked, as they observed the practices of the pagan nations surrounding them, "Shall I even offer my firstborn for my transgression, the fruit of my body for the sin of my soul?" Perhaps the only way to appease the anger of God was by offering a human sacrifice. What might bring God pleasure? If not a ram, calf, or rivers of oil, perhaps it was the very life of their firstborn that was required.

God made clear stipulations in the law and spelled out precisely what was expected when the people of God came to the temple to worship the Most High. Yet it wasn't enough to simply bring the right sacrifices to God in worship. The truth is, while these offerings were important instruments of worship, God was requiring more—something that would be expressed in the lives of God's people outside the confines of the temple. Through the words of the prophet, this something more was clearly stated: "God has shown you what is good: to act justly and to love mercy and to walk humbly with your God." These attitudes and actions are more than theological concepts, and they are more than good intentions. This is what the Lord requires.

The Power of Three

I love Venn diagrams. Designed by British philosopher John Venn in 1880, his model of interlocking circles illustrates simple sets of relationships and all the possible connection points.

Since that day people have been using his diagram to visually capture just about everything of importance in the universe.

Have you ever considered how many significant things in the Christian faith involve sets of three?

The Father, Son, and Holy Spirit
Body, soul, and spirit
Faith, hope, and love

When it comes to worship, the prophet Micah would have done well with a Venn diagram in hand, for the Lord requires three interrelated things: justice, mercy and humility. And the reason God requires these things is because they are deeply connected to the nature and character of God. God is a god of justice, mercy, and humility.

The God of Justice

The story of God begins in Genesis 1 with the creation of a good world—mark that—a very good world. God creates everything in heaven and on earth and declares that it is very good. This includes the lights that fill the heavens, the living things that occupy the seas, skies, and dry land, and ultimately the crown of creation—humankind. In those opening chapters, all was well. A brief description of the state of the creation might go as follows:

In the beginning, God and humanity experienced intimacy, communion, and friendship. Humanity lived in oneness with God and with one another, and the entire created order was marked by harmony and peace.

This is the world as it ought to be.

Yet brokenness and alienation creep into this good creation, and the reality of sin distorts all the goodness that God has built into the world. The intimacy, communion, and friendship between God and humanity is broken; the oneness of humanity is disrupted, and the harmony and peace within the created order is shattered. We call this chapter in the story "the Fall."

Now it only takes a few moments to realize that we are living in the midst of a fallen world. Scan the headlines, consider the latest natural disaster, or look within your own heart; and you will have to admit that things are not the way they ought to be.

One of the clearest signs of the fall is injustice. Every day, people experience the reality of economic injustice, gender injustice, and racial and ethnic injustice. Because of the fall, people do not receive what is right and just. Workers do not receive just compensation for their labor. Children die from preventable diseases. Girls around the globe are locked into oppressive systems because they do not have access to education and training. Individuals and organizations seeking only their own good, profit, or comfort cause great damage to the environment. These things grieve the heart of God.

New Testament scholar and theologian N. T. Wright describes the mission of God as setting the world right. This mission flows directly from God's nature and character. Because God is just, God is committed to making all things right in the world. This is ultimately accomplished through the redemptive work of Christ. In Colossians 1, the Apostle Paul describes the cosmic dimensions of the work of Jesus: "For God was pleased to have all his fullness dwell in him, and through him to reconcile to himself all things, whether things on earth or things in heaven, by making peace through his blood, shed on the cross" (1:19–20).

Jesus offers his life as the perfect sacrifice for sin, and through his death and resurrection, God is reconciling all things. Intimacy, communion, and friendship between God and humanity become possible again. Oneness between people can be restored. And God's people can help this good creation once again flourish and thrive. God does not leave the world in its sin and brokenness. God redeems, restores, and renews. God is setting the world right through Christ. God is a God of justice.

As people who bear the image of our creator, we too are called to the work of justice. God invites you and me to participate, to join in this work of justice.

What does God require of us? To act justly.

The God of Mercy

The second thing that God requires is mercy. Let's be honest: mercy as a personal or corporate attribute does not have the best reputation. Mercy is often considered a weaker, emotional characteristic that powerful and competent people do not exhibit or exercise.

Why does God require mercy? Because God is merciful.

In Psalm 145, David writes of God's greatness and power, splendor and majesty, and God's goodness and compassion:

> *Great is the Lord and most worthy of praise;*
> *his greatness no one can fathom.*
> *One generation commends your works to another;*
> *they tell of your mighty acts.*
> *They speak of the glorious splendor of your majesty—*
> *and I will meditate on your wonderful works.*
> *They tell of the power of your awesome works—*
> *and I will proclaim your great deeds.*
> *They celebrate your abundant goodness*
> *and joyfully sing of your righteousness.*
> *The Lord is gracious and compassionate,*
> *slow to anger and rich in love.*
> *The Lord is good to all;*
> *he has compassion on all he has made. (vv. 3–9)*

The Hebrew word for compassion used in this text is a potent one. Andrew Purves writes:

> *The Hebrew word for compassion is* rachamin. *It certainly describes a powerful emotion of deep concern for the welfare of another. Unlike our common connection of an emotion with the heart, however, the Hebrews connected emotions with the lower viscera, the organs located in the abdominal cavity. The innards or bowels were the seat of the sympathetic emotions in general. In their customary physical, fleshy way, the Hebrews, when they felt emotions, felt them deeply in their bodies.*

There is yet another element to rachamin, however, which particularizes the seat of compassion in a quite remarkable way. Rachamin is derived from another Hebrew word, rechem, which means womb or uterus. The literal meaning of compassion then, is the womb pained in solidarity with the suffering of another. The feeling of deep kinship with another is now understood in an intimate and physical way as the wounding of the womb. The wounded womb is the core of the biblical meaning of compassion.

At its most basic, compassion represents a feminine characteristic of God, if it is appropriate to speak of God in such anthropomorphic language. Compassion describes God's mothering solidarity with God's people. The notion of God's compassion as the wounding of the womb of God is a somewhat unnerving notion, and one a man may only approach with some sensitivity due to the fact that the reference is quite beyond his biological experience. Indeed, to speak of the inner experience of God here as the wounding of God's womb is quite beyond any human imagining. Yet the biblical image of compassion compels us to suggest that it refers to God's deepest and most creative—we might even say life-giving—suffering with the people. There is great beauty in the image and great pathos.[1]

While I agree with Purves that, as a male, this understanding of compassion is beyond my biological experience, I have learned about this emotional dimension by observing the way my wife as the mother of our children relates to them. While my relationship

---

[1] Andrew Purves, *The Search for Compassion* (Louisville: Westminster John Knox Press, 1989), 68–69.

to our children is a strong one, my wife's connection goes deeper—it is visceral and womb-like—and she suffers with them and experiences their pain at a level that is both beautiful and heartbreaking. How much more does God feel the pain and suffering of God's children!

The New Testament builds on the Old Testament understanding of God's compassion as it describes both the character and activity of Jesus:

> *When Jesus landed and saw a large crowd, he had compassion on them, because they were like sheep without a shepherd. So he began teaching them many things. (Mark 6:34)*

> *Jesus went through all the towns and villages, teaching in their synagogues, proclaiming the good news of the kingdom and healing every disease and sickness. When he saw the crowds, he had compassion on them, because they were harassed and helpless, like sheep without a shepherd. (Matthew 9:35–36)*

> *Jesus had compassion on them and touched their eyes. Immediately they received their sight and followed him. (Matthew 20:34)*

Look closely at these examples. Jesus is touched emotionally in the depth of his being, and this emotion moves him into action: lost and harassed sheep are shepherded, the sick are healed, and the blind receive sight.

In the Gospels, the word compassion is used only in reference to Jesus and two other characters, the Good Samaritan in Luke 10 and the Prodigal Father in Luke 15. In both of these parables, Jesus once again connects the emotion of compassion with practical actions as the Samaritan meets the physical needs of the injured person and the father runs to welcome and restore his lost son.

Justice and compassion must go hand in hand. There is a synergy between mercy and justice. When we see injustice in the world, feel it in the depth of our being, and then act in ways that bring hope and comfort, we are indeed doing what the Lord requires.

Acting justly and loving mercy are more than theological concepts; they are convictions that God wants us to flesh out in our life. Bono from U2 has waxed poetically on the relationship between justice and compassion, and he uses the word charity to describe a love motivated by a faith in a God who loves us and then calls us to love others. Bono has critiqued and challenged the church to do more than just be a compassionate, charitable people. During his speech at the National Prayer Breakfast on February 2, 2006, he said, "It's not about charity at all, is it? It's about justice. Let me repeat that: It's not about charity at all. It's about justice. And that's too bad. Because you're good at charity. Americans, like the Irish, are good at it. We like to give, and we give a lot, even those who can't afford it. But justice is a higher standard."

Charity is incomplete apart from justice. Charity, mercy, and compassion will never be enough to bring healing to our broken world. There is a higher call—a calling to connect compassion, mercy, and charity with justice.

Jeff Goins has written a brilliant book called *Wrecked: When a Broken World Slams into Your Comfortable Life.* What do you think of when you hear the word wrecked? Have you ever heard somebody say that, "I've been wrecked?" Have you ever been wrecked?"

"To be wrecked," Goins writes, "is to be disabused of the status quo. It means to have a transformation that goes beyond mere words, to be introduced to another way of life, to follow in the footsteps of a teacher who is calling you through the eye of a needle. Often it involves being catalyzed by an encounter with pain."[2]

While the process of being wrecked can be a horrible, ugly, and gut-wrenching experience, it can be breathtakingly beautiful and liberating as well. Being wrecked is a difficult and painful process, but one that is necessary if we are going to become the kind of people who do what God requires.

During my graduate studies in the 1980s, one of the most significant geo-political issues facing the church was the policy of apartheid in South Africa. Leaders from that nation, both black and white, would often visit our campus, speaking passionately and prophetically concerning the injustices occurring in their country. For the first time in my life, I began to think about the implications that faith has on everyday, ordinary issues of public policy and economics. As I listened to the stories of injustice and suffering, my heart was moved. My life was being wrecked.

I clearly remember the moment the issue moved from the abstract to the concrete in my life. One Wednesday morning during our weekly chapel service, Allan Boesak, a visiting preacher from South Africa, challenged the worshipping community (students, faculty, and administration alike) to consider our financial investments. He said, "Examine your investments. Look at what and where you are investing your money." Boesak was addressing a movement in which American

---

[2] Jeff Goins, *Wrecked: When a Broken World Slams into Your Comfortable Life* (Chicago: Moody Press, 2012), 30.

companies and pension plans divested their investments in South African companies. This act of justice and the resulting economic pressure caused the South African government to reevaluate its position and eventually change its policies and eliminate apartheid in South Africa. Hearing the stories of men and women who suffered greatly because of the inhumane and unjust policies wrecked me. My life would never be the same.

A few years later, I had the opportunity to travel to Mexico City and serve the massive population of that city that calls the garage dump home. Visiting the garbage dumps and witnessing the poverty, pain, suffering, hunger, and complete lack of access to anything life-giving absolutely wrecked me.

After that first gut-wrenching trip to Mexico City, upon my late-night arrival at home, I tiptoed into my daughter's bedroom just to get a glimpse of her face and gently kiss her forehead. When I saw my daughter, I saw in her face the faces of the Mexican children I had left behind, and I began to weep uncontrollably. The poverty and the pain wrecked me. I simply was unable to put these worlds together.

What does the Lord require of us? To act justly and to love mercy. Mercy alone will not heal the brokenness of our world.

Our community of faith partners with a local church that serves the poor and vulnerable population that lives on the streets of Pittsburgh. Every other month we join them on a Sunday evening, and after worshiping together, we serve them a hot, nutritious meal. I love the fact that through our presence and the gift of food, we are bringing real help and hope to people in real need. We are putting our faith into action. But it's not enough. Why are there homeless people? How can it be that in a city that is flourishing and prospering, there are men and women—many of whom have faithfully served our nation in the military—who now find themselves homeless? Have we stopped to consider the economic and sociological issues that cause homelessness in the first place? We can serve meals day after day, but there is a deeper justice issue underneath it all. We need to start rolling up our sleeves and asking the question, "Why?" What can we do to change the way things are in our world so that men and women, boys and girls will have a place to call home along with access to food, education, and jobs?

I believe in the power of partnerships, and our church currently sponsors about eighty children in East Africa through a partnership with World Vision and Compassion International. Every month as checks are written and bank accounts debited, these acts of compassion bring real help and hope to children in real need. But there are larger issues at play. During a recent trip to Uganda, I discovered that almost 400 people in that country (many of them children) die every day from malaria, a disease that happens to be preventable and treatable. I also learned that throwing large amounts of money at the problem is not necessarily the answer. There are plenty of mosquito nets in Uganda, and in many communities, life-saving medications are available that can treat the disease. Why then does this disease continue to kill so many people? I believe the answer to that question involves justice. For instance, why can't the people who need the nets or medication obtain access to them? What drives people who may have mosquito nets to use them to protect their cattle rather than their children? Why are they not educated and sensitized to how best prevent or treat the disease?

I have a friend who is incredibly bright and theologically savvy. He is discerning God's call on his life, and right now, as he awaits a call to a pastoral position with a local church, he is working in an upscale, eco-friendly grocery store. Recently Karlin relayed to me how he has been wrecked when it comes to the whole food industry, particularly the issues underlying the whole food ecosystem. Over a cup of coffee, he said, "Terry, be very careful about the coffee you drink and the chocolate you eat. There are issues of justice underneath them. Of all the food products we consume, chocolate and coffee have the most issues of oppression, exploitation, all sorts of crazy and evil things attached to them." The coffee we drink, the chocolate we eat, the clothes we wear—all of these involve issues of justice and compassion.

What does the Lord require of us? To act justly and to love mercy.

The God of Humility

Let me complete the Venn diagram by delving into the third thing the Lord requires: humility. One of the most powerful examples of humanity that the world has ever witnessed is described in Philippians 2:

> In your relationships with one another, have the same mindset as Christ Jesus: Who, being in very nature God, did not consider equality with God something to be used to his own advantage; rather, he made himself nothing by taking the very nature of a servant, being made in human likeness. And being found in appearance as a man, he humbled himself by becoming obedient to death—even death on a cross! (vv. 2:5–8)

This passage has long been known as "the kenosis," drawing upon the Greek word used to describe both the attitude and action of Jesus. The eternal Son of God, second person of the Trinity, willingly chooses to divest himself of his divine prerogative and comes to earth. Here is how two early church fathers explain Jesus' pathway of humility:

> *Jesus did not take on his humanity in the simple way that a person puts on clothes, as something exterior to him. Rather he took on human form in a manner inexpressibly more excellent and more intimate than that. The apostle has made it sufficiently clear what he meant by He was made to appear in human likeness. He was not exhaustively reduced to being a man. He rather assumed the true human estate when he put on the man.*[3]

> *Read the record of his compassion. It pleased him, being the Word of God, to take the form of a slave. So he willed to be joined to our common human condition. He took to himself the toils of the members who suffer. He suffered and toiled on our behalf. This is in accord with his great love of humankind.*[4]

Jesus sets his robes of majesty aside, clothes himself with flesh and blood, and enters into our world. The English Standard Version states that Jesus, "though he was in the form of God, did not count equality with God a thing to be grasped" (Philippians 2:6, ESV). In other words, while Jesus had every right to exert every molecule of divinity and demand that the universe bend to his will, instead—motivated by love—he chose to humble himself and sacrificially offer his life back to God on behalf of all humankind.

---

[3] Augustine as quoted in Mark J. Edwards, *Galatians, Ephesians, Philippians* (ACCS 8; Downers Grove: InterVarsity, 1999) 248.

[4] Eusebius of Caesarea as quoted in Mark J. Edwards, *Galatians, Ephesians, Philippians* (ACCS 8; Downers Grove: InterVarsity, 1999), 246–247.

C. S. Lewis said, "Humility is not thinking less of yourself; humility is thinking of yourself less." Jesus knew exactly who he was, and his strong sense of identity empowered him to offer up his life for the sake of the world. It can do the same for us as well. Walking humbly with our God demands a healthy and accurate self-understanding. We are God's handiwork, beautifully created in the image of God to reflect God's image to the world. We are broken, deeply flawed, sinful creatures who fail to love God completely and our neighbors compassionately.

This is where a robust understanding of the gospel comes into play. In some circles there seems to be an overly optimistic understanding of humanity. This group draws deeply from the creation narrative outlined in the first two chapters of Genesis. They would say, "Look at the power and possibilities of the creation narrative. Through our human efforts, we can eliminate injustice in the world and usher in the kingdom of God here on earth. We can get back to the Garden. By working together, we can change the world."

Others bristle at that viewpoint of humanity. This group picks up the narrative in Genesis 3, traditionally known as "the Fall," where we find humanity rebelling against its creator. This group might describe humanity as "nothing but wretched worms." Adam and Eve placed themselves at the center of the universe, intending to create a world for themselves, refusing to be satisfied with the life that God offered. This was the grand tragedy of the Garden, and it is a story that plays itself out in our world on a daily basis. As Rob Bell says in his Nooma video *Trees*, "The tragedy is not so much that Genesis 3 happened, but that it happens."

Which narrative is accurate? Which storyline represents reality?

Of course it is not an either/or deal. The truth is found in a both/and understanding of these narratives: we are beautiful and broken. We are fearfully and wonderfully created in the image of God. And yet, we are willful sinners who not only think too highly of ourselves but also think of ourselves much too often. To walk humbly with our God is to embrace the truth that men and women together image God to the world, while also acknowledging our deep need for the grace of God in Jesus Christ. Our humble Savior, Jesus the Christ, is a constant and faithful reminder that God will not leave us or this world in its brokenness, but, through the power of Jesus' life-giving death on the cross, is renewing us and calling us to be his agents in the world. We are not only beneficiaries of God's grace in Jesus Christ; we are agents of God's grace and goodness in the world. Apart from Christ, we can do nothing; connected to Jesus, we can accomplish anything and everything God seeks to do in, with and through us.

In his song "Wholly Yours," David Crowder sums up this reality by using images of dirt and divinity. We are people created from the dust of the earth and yet filled with the divine breath of God (Genesis 2:7). Or as the Apostle Paul states, we are earthen vessels, entrusted with the treasure of the good news of Jesus Christ (2 Corinthians 4:7). Amazing!

The Lord requires humility because God is a God of humility.

The Micah Challenge

Micah Challenge (www.micahchallengeusa.org) is a global Christian campaign to end extreme poverty. Inspired by Scripture, guided by the Holy Spirit, and covered in prayer, this group advocates for a more just world. Its members are convinced that extreme poverty and hunger will not be overcome by securing more food, but rather by securing more justice. This motivates them to engage in transformational advocacy, an activity they define as "the process of challenging ourselves and our leaders to change behavior, policies, and attitudes that perpetuate injustice and deny God's will for human flourishing."

Over a cup of coffee (fair trade, of course), I had an engaging conversation with Jason, a passionate young leader who serves as the director of Micah Challenge. As the son of Egyptian immigrants, he was compelled by the plight of the persecuted church in Egypt to enter the struggle for justice. His hunger and thirst for justice are palpable. It is clear that the motivating force in Jason's life is not a political agenda or economic ideology. His commitment to justice and his devotion to helping others engage in this cause are guided by these ancient words:

> With what shall I come before the Lord
> and bow down before the exalted God?
> Shall I come before him with burnt offerings,
> with calves a year old?
> Will the Lord be pleased with thousands of rams,
> with ten thousand rivers of olive oil?
> Shall I offer my firstborn for my transgression,
> the fruit of my body for the sin of my soul?
> He has shown you, O mortal, what is good.
> And what does the Lord require of you?
> To act justly and to love mercy
> and to walk humbly with your God. (Micah 6:6–8)

What does the Lord require? Three things: to act justly, to love mercy, and to walk humbly with our God. The intersection of justice, mercy, and humility becomes the sweet spot of worship.

Honestly, life with God would be simpler if the requirement was the sacrifice of a ram or cow, or the offering of a thousand gallons of the finest olive oil. While it would make quite a mess in our sanctuaries, at least we could walk away from that activity with the confidence that we had done what the Lord had required. We make our offerings, which in turn make us good to go, and then get on with the rest of our lives. The truth that flows from the lips of Micah is a challenging one: it is impossible to fulfill your obligations in an hour on Sunday morning. It is impossible to complete your requirements with an offering left on the altar. God wants our lives twenty-four hours a day, seven days a week, 365 days a year. Acting justly, loving mercy, and walking in humility—day in and day out—is what the Lord requires of us.

I am sure you have heard the apocryphal tale of the child, the elderly man, and the starfish. While walking along a beach, an elderly man saw a young boy in the distance who was picking up starfish off the sand and gently tossing them back into the ocean. As he neared the boy, the man smiled and said, "Why are you throwing starfish back into the water?"

The boy replied, "The sun is up, and the tide is going out; if I do not throw them back in, they will die."

The man commented, "But, son, don't you realize that so many starfish wash up along every mile of this beach? You cannot possibly make a difference!"

The boy listened politely. He then bent down, gently picked up another starfish and tossed it past the breaking waves. "Sir," he replied, "I made a difference to that one."

This past summer, while riding my bike along the edge of the Atlantic Ocean in Hilton Head, South Carolina, I witnessed this story being played out in real time. It was low tide, and there were hundreds of starfish grounded on the beach. Right before my eyes there was a small group of people picking up the starfish and gently returning them to the ocean.

The challenge to act justly, love mercy, and walk humbly can be overwhelming. With so much brokenness and need in the world, is it possible to make a real difference? At times I have no idea where to begin. In those moments, I remember to pick up the closest starfish and return it to the water. Daily, through continual prayer and discernment, I am asking God to show me what it would mean for my life to be an intersection of justice, mercy, and humility.

Perhaps it begins with the coffee we drink or the chocolate we eat. Maybe it involves the clothes in our closets or the investments in our 401(k). It might entail serving a meal to the homeless and learning more about the causes of homelessness in our city, and then advocating for real change. It might mean writing a monthly check to sponsor a child in the developing world and exploring the root issues of poverty, hunger, and disease.

What would it look like in your life to take the challenge issued by the prophet Micah? For this is what the Lord requires. This is true worship. This is the holy work that God calls us to live into each and every day in the places where we live, learn, and labor. For justice, mercy, and humility are signposts of the kingdom that is both here and yet to come. To this holy work we now turn our attention.

worship in the new creation

The mission of the church is nothing more or less than the outworking, in the power of the Spirit, of Jesus' bodily resurrection. It is the anticipation of the time when God will fill the earth with his glory, transform the old heavens and earth into the new, and raise his children from the dead to populate and rule over the redeemed world he has made.

–N. T. Wright

Heaven Is for Real: A Little Boy's Astounding Story of His Trip to Heaven and Back has been one of the best-selling books in the Christian circles over the past decade. In this book, pastor Todd Burpo reports on the near-death experience of his then four-year-old son Colton, who shares of meeting Jesus in heaven (as well as a number of his deceased relatives) after undergoing emergency surgery in 2003. This book has sold over seven million copies, and recently, the movie based upon this book was released into theaters and generated almost $30 million in revenue.

In both my personal and pastoral experience, I have discovered that people are curious about the afterlife and questions abound. Where is heaven? What is heaven? How does a person get into heaven? What will happen in heaven? Throughout the ages, heaven has been a controversial subject and it continues to be in our day. What about you? What has shaped your vision of heaven and formed your understanding of the afterlife? Unfortunately, it seems that many today have been more informed by popular culture than by a robust exploration of the Scriptures.

In this final chapter, I will advance the idea that the work of worship will continue in heaven. In fact, three things will remain when the new creation comes in its fullness: the work of worship, life in the beloved community, and a feast.

A Vision of Heaven

I once heard a well-known pastor and author introduce his director of music and worship leader with these words: "This man has eternal job security. In heaven, my job will be finished because preaching will cease, but music will continue forever and ever."

For many, heaven is viewed as an endless praise and worship service, complete with both angelic and human choirs and the casting of crowns. The book of Revelation provides a glimpse of this eternal activity:

> *Day and night they never stop saying: "Holy, holy, holy is the Lord God Almighty, who was, and is, and is to come." Whenever the living creatures give glory, honor*

and thanks to him who sits on the throne and who lives forever and ever, the twenty-four elders fall down before him who sits on the throne and worship him who lives forever and ever. They lay their crowns before the throne and say: "You are worthy, our Lord and God, to receive glory and honor and power, for you created all things, and by your will they were created and have their being." (Revelation 4:9–11)

And in Revelation 5:

And they sang a new song, saying: "You are worthy to take the scroll and to open its seals, because you were slain, and with your blood you purchased for God persons from every tribe and language and people and nation. You have made them to be a kingdom and priests to serve our God, and they will reign on the earth." Then I looked and heard the voice of many angels, numbering thousands upon thousands, and ten thousand times ten thousand. They encircled the throne and the living creatures and the elders. In a loud voice they were saying:

"Worthy is the Lamb, who was slain, to receive power and wealth and wisdom and strength and honor and glory and praise!"

Then I heard every creature in heaven and on earth and under the earth and on the sea, and all that is in them, saying:

"To him who sits on the throne and to the Lamb be praise and honor and glory and power, for ever and ever!" The four living creatures said, "Amen," and the elders fell down and worshiped. (vv. 9–14)

This picture of heavenly worship is a moving one. The entire creation recognizes and acknowledges the holiness of God and the reality that Jesus, the Lamb of God, is indeed the one worthy of our eternal adoration. Throughout history, the people of God have gathered in places as diverse as majestic cathedrals, school gymnasiums, and individual homes, lifting their voices with these expressions of worship, thereby joining the eternal activity of heaven.

As much as I appreciate music and understand the power of corporate singing, I find it difficult to imagine that this will be the only activity in the new creation. To be honest, this sounds to me on the boring side. While lifting our voices in adoration to our God and Savior will certainly be one dimension of worship in the new creation, the Scriptures provide a more robust picture of heaven and the eternal activities.

The Grand Narrative

Recently I gathered with four hundred other people to celebrate the work of the Coalition for Christian Outreach (CCO) (www.ccojubilee.org). The CCO is a campus ministry that partners with churches, colleges, and other organizations to develop men and women who live out their Christian faith in every area of life. Their mission is summarized with these words: "Transforming college students to transform the world." The work they engage in is transformational in nature, and the CCO staff challenges the students they serve to submit every area of their lives to Jesus Christ because all things belong to God. Our community of faith is privileged to partner with the CCO on two local campuses—Point Park University and the University of Pittsburgh's Medical and Dental School.

At this gala celebration, there were scattered around the room large banners with images of students the CCO serves. Emblazoned on these banners were phrases such as Education Matters. Nursing Matters. Engineering Matters. Mathematics Matters. Chemistry Matters. Social Work Matters.

These banners were designed to make a bold statement: if Jesus Christ is Lord of all, then every dimension of life matters, not only now, but forever. The CCO calls this the Jubilee vision, a vision deeply rooted in the grand narrative of the Scriptures that tells the story of creation, fall, redemption, and restoration. Following is a brief summary of the four movements, or chapters, in this story of all stories.

Creation

In this opening movement we discover that the triune God is not only the creator of all things, but the one who sustains the creation as well. Since God is the creator, God is the one who gives meaning and purpose to everything that exists, and in fact, is the one for whom everything exists. The creation is good, indeed it is very good, and every dimension of it reflects God's glory. Humanity was created in the image of God and entrusted with the responsibility to care for the creation and to work with it to help the creation flourish and become everything God intended it to be.

The Creation chapter of the story reveals the world as it OUGHT to be.

Fall

The second movement is the Fall, the chapter in which God's image bearers rebelled against their creator, alienating themselves from God, from one another, and from the entire created universe. As a result, God's good and beautiful creation was marred by sin's ugliness and all its unintended consequences. As Rob Bell says in his *NOOMA®* video "Trees," "Maybe the truth of the Adam and Eve story, maybe the greatest power of the story, is not so much that it happened, but that it happens."[1] While the first plot movement, Creation, illustrates God's ideal, the second plot movement, the Fall, portrays the world as we know it today. The universal flourishing and mutual interdependence of God's original creation was broken as humanity's sin introduced disarray and disorder.

The Fall chapter reveals the world as it IS.

Redemption

Since humanity rebelled against God, God is the only one who can rescue us from our sinful state. Early in the story, God spoke hopeful words to Adam and Eve and to future generations that foreshadowed the ultimate plan and agent of redemption. This rescuer and redeemer is Jesus Christ. There is no other hope for being rescued and redeemed for God outside of Jesus and his work, for "salvation is found in no one else, for there is no other name given under heaven by which we must be saved" (Acts 4:12). While the salvation of humanity stands at the center of God's redemptive purposes, God does not limit redemption to the divine image bearers. In Colossians 1, the Apostle Paul outlined the cosmic scope of Christ's redemptive work: "For God was pleased to have all his fullness dwell in him, and through him to reconcile to himself all things, whether things on earth or things in heaven, by making peace through his blood, shed on the cross" (Colossians 1:19–20).

[1] Rob Bell, "Trees," *NOOMA®* (Grand Rapids, Michigan: Flannel, 2005).

The Redemption chapter reveals what the world CAN be through Jesus Christ.

Restoration

The plan of God culminates with both a people redeemed for God and a new heaven and new earth, a place where sin and death and their consequences are completely removed. Love defines how this redeemed people will relate to God, one another, and indeed the entire new creation. God's redemptive work through Christ extends through God's people to God's cosmos, so that in the end "creation itself will be set free from its bondage to decay and obtain the freedom of the glory of the children of God" (Romans 8:21). One day Jesus will establish the kingdom in its fullness, bringing with it the renewal and restoration of all things. As we anticipate this future, we participate now in the work of restoration by serving as agents of reconciliation. Every restorative action provides a foretaste of this future reality.

The Restoration chapter reveals the world as it WILL be.

This is, as N. T. Wright says, "the true story for the entire world," and this restoration chapter is the rightful place to conclude this book.

The Coming Kingdom

The final book in the Bible, Revelation, provides a number of compelling images of the coming kingdom. However, our understanding of the world to come is not limited to Revelation. Tucked away in Scripture, God has provided many other passages that give a glimpse of the future, most notably in the prophetic writings of the Old Testament. A faithful reading of the Scriptures demands that we take the various threads that appear throughout the testaments and weave them together into a glorious and holistic understanding of the coming kingdom. This approach enlarges our imagination and fuels us to live with a greater sense of kingdom urgency.

In Isaiah 60, the prophet paints a beautiful picture of the coming kingdom:

> *Arise, shine, for your light has come, and the glory of the Lord rises upon you. See, darkness covers the earth and thick darkness is over the peoples, but the Lord rises upon you and his glory appears over you. Nations will come to your light, and kings to the brightness of your dawn. Lift up your eyes and look about you: All assemble and come to you; your sons come from afar, and your daughters are carried on the hip. Then you will look and be radiant, your heart will throb and swell with joy; the wealth on the seas will be brought to you, to you the riches of the nations will come. (vv. 1–5)*

> *Surely the islands look to me; in the lead are the ships of Tarshish, bringing your children from afar, with their silver and gold, to the honor of the Lord your God, the Holy One of Israel, for he has endowed you with splendor. Foreigners will rebuild your walls, and their kings will serve you. Though in anger I struck you, in favor I will show you compassion. Your gates will always stand open, they will never be shut, day or night, so that people may bring you the wealth of the nations—their kings led in triumphal procession. (vv. 9–11)*

When the kingdom comes in its fullness, the nations of the world will be attracted to the glory that resides among God's people. Not only will they come, they will bring with them their wealth and riches. The prophet describes the ships of Tarshish as carrying precious cargo to the New Jerusalem, not only sons and daughters but silver and gold as well.

What are we to make of the wealth and riches of the nations? What role will the silver and gold that is carried by the pagan ships play in the new creation? Could God and would God choose to use the affluence of the nations as part of the new creation? In his book *When the Kings Come Marching In: Isaiah and the New Jerusalem*, Richard Mouw writes:

> Not all of the items of pagan culture will be gathered as it is into the Holy City. A pagan ship will be changed into a routine ship but it will still be a ship. But other things will have to have their identities, basic functions, transformed; some of them will be changed almost beyond recognition. Swords will become plowshares. Spears will be changed into pruning hooks. Racist posters will become aesthetic objects that will enhance the beauty of the city. Perhaps missiles will become play areas for children. Once again, the emphasis here is on transformation, not destruction. God is still pictured as working with the filling of creation... What applies on this level of personal destiny seems to hold true also for the whole creation, including its cultural dimensions. God will work with what he has created and with the filling that human beings have added to what he made in the beginning. The fruits of history, even sinful history, will be gathered into the City, and made into fitting vessels of service.[2]

---

[2] Richard Mouw, *When the Kings Come Marching In: Isaiah and the New Jerusalem* (Grand Rapids: Wm. B. Eerdmans, revised edition, 2002), 40–41.

What might this look like, and what implications might this have for God's people in the days to come? If engineering matters to God, perhaps in the new creation, engineers will build the streets of gold and the infrastructure that will support the Holy City. If mathematics matters to God, perhaps in the new creation, mathematicians will uncover new formulas and proofs. If chemistry matters to God, perhaps chemists will discover new elements and ways to use these discoveries to promote flourishing and life. If music matters to God, musicians may uncover new tonalities or chord progressions that will contribute to the aesthetic fabric of the Holy City.

Imagine having the time to learn a new language—Portuguese, Swahili or Mandarin. Or the time to learn to play the cello, tenor sax, or xylophone. What kind of art will be created in the coming kingdom as artists have unlimited time to create works of beauty—paintings, films, drama, and music? What might play and recreation look like without an unhealthy sense of win-at-all-costs mentality? Imagine playing an intense, competitive nine innings of baseball and at the end of it all saying to your fellow players, "See you tomorrow; let's do it all over again."

Imagine relationships without strife, competitiveness, and division. While I am not exactly sure what work counselors, therapists, and social workers will engage in the new kingdom, I suspect it will in some way involve helping us enjoy fully the new and renewed relationships we will have.

In the new creation, the curse of the fall will be completely reversed. As God's people, we will join with our Creator and Redeemer, bringing everything we possess and submitting it fully to the glory of God and the Holy City. As Craig Bartholomew and Michael Goheen write:

> The physical reunification of heaven and earth is a dramatic picture of the restored peace and harmony between the Creator and creation. God comes to dwell on the new earth with humankind, removing sin and all its effects. There's no more sickness, pain, or death because the relationship between God and humankind has been healed. God is once again as close to us as in the days when he walked with Adam and Eve in the garden. Relationships among human beings have been healed: love reigns. The whole of human life is purified, and even the nonhuman creation shares in this liberation from its former slavery to sin and death. Here's the stunning goal and destiny of the biblical story, the true story of the whole world; a renewed creation—healed, redeemed, and restored.[3]

Imagine living in neighborhoods without strife, violence, and fear. One of my favorite organizations in our city is The Pittsburgh Project, a Christian nonprofit community development organization with a thirty-year track record of developing servant leaders and serving the city's most vulnerable residents (www.pittsburghproject.org). Groups from around the county come to Pittsburgh during the summer months to partner with The Pittsburgh Project in bringing real help and hope to people in real need. These groups perform free home repairs for more than two hundred of Pittsburgh's elderly homeowners and help to spearhead economic development and job training efforts in our Pittsburgh neighborhoods.

---

[3] Craig G. Bartholomew and Michael W. Goheen. *The True Story of the Whole World: Finding Your Place in the Biblical Drama* (Grand Rapids: Faith Alive Christian Resources, 2009), 167.

What motivates The Pittsburgh Project to do what it does? Its organizational vision is captured in these words: "Our vision is that Pittsburgh will be called a City of Truth, where once again men and women of ripe old age will sit in the streets each with cane in hand because of age, and where the city streets will be filled with boys and girls playing there." When I first heard those words, I confess that I thought they seemed to form a rather odd vision statement. And then I realized that the statement flowed from a vision the Old Testament prophet Zechariah had of life in the new creation:

> *This is what the LORD says: "I will return to Zion and dwell in Jerusalem. Then Jerusalem will be called the Faithful City, and the mountain of the LORD Almighty will be called the Holy Mountain." This is what the LORD Almighty says: "Once again men and women of ripe old age will sit in the streets of Jerusalem, each of them with cane in hand because of their age. The city streets will be filled with boys and girls playing there."* (Zechariah 8:3–5)

The second-century church father Irenaeus said, "The glory of God is a human being fully alive." When the kingdom of God comes in its fullness, we will be fully alive, and this dynamic new life will include the work of worship. This is the Jubilee vision— this is worship. This is a vision of heaven that is never boring, one that is always dynamic and consistent with the arc of the grand narrative of God's salvation history.

Now, we offer our lives back to God for the life of the world. In the new creation, we will offer our lives to God for the life of the beloved community.

Living Now in Light of Then

In May 2014, the world mourned the death of the beloved American poet Maya Angelou. This remarkable woman's words were a source of inspiration for many, but perhaps more inspiring than her words was her robust approach to life. Angelou was a shining example of a human being who was fully alive.

As a tribute to this remarkable life, Jana Riess wrote a fascinating blog post entitled, "Maya Angelou Is Not in Heaven." I love the way Riess describes Angelou's life:

> Over the last 24 hours I've seen several people refer to Angelou as the "caged bird" of her writings. She is now free, they suggest—free of the mortal body that caged her, that cages us all. Death has released her, and now she is in heaven. I beg to differ. Angelou is not in heaven "now." Her writings show a joyful person who was never not in heaven. To me, an ongoing theme of her remarkable work has always been its full-on, all-in commitment to living life in the kingdom. That's God's kingdom in the here and now. Angelou wasn't waiting for some pie-in-the-sky release to an ethereal realm.[4]

What does it look like to live in this present moment in light of the time when God's kingdom will come in its fullness? For some, the goal of the Christian life for some is to faithfully depart this world and go to heaven, the place where eternal life really begins. My reading of Scripture presents a different perspective: the objective of the life of faith is not to be removed from this life

---

[4] Jana Riess, "Maya Angelou Is Not in Heaven," *Flunking Sainthood* (blog), May 25, 2014, http://janariess.religionnews.com/2014/05/29/maya-angelou-heaven/.

and this earth, but rather to live now in light of then, to live here in light of there.

Remember the liturgical calendar? I am writing these words on the Monday after the third Sunday of Easter. I love the fact that, historically, church has viewed Easter as much more than a single day or event. Easter is not only a season, but also an entirely new way to understand our life both individually and as members of the community of faith. It presents a fresh framework of hope. As N. T. Wright says, "Easter was when Hope in person surprised the whole world by coming forward from the future into the present…Jesus' resurrection is the beginning of God's new project not to snatch people away from earth to heaven but to colonize earth with the life of heaven. That, after all, is what the Lord's Prayer is about."[5]

"On earth as it is in heaven." That phrase from the lips of Jesus has the potential to change the way we live, relate, and worship. I once heard the wise, spiritual formation teacher and author Dallas Willard paraphrase this petition with these simple words, "God, bring up there, down here."

A friend of mine, Josh, fronts a band that makes delightful music that speaks of a world of which we can only dream. They call themselves "Colonizing the Cosmos." Isn't that a fantastic name? This is a beautiful description of how God invites us to live as redeemed people right here, right now. We are called to colonize this earth with the life of heaven. This is nothing less than living into God's grand mission for the world. Again, to quote Wright:

---

[5] N. T. Wright, *Surprised by Hope: Rethinking Heaven, the Resurrection and the Mission of the Church* (New York: HarperOne, 2008), 29.

The mission of the church is nothing more or less than the outworking, in the power of the Spirit, of Jesus' bodily resurrection. It is the anticipation of the time when God will fill the earth with his glory, transform the old heavens and earth into the new, and raise his children from the dead to populate and rule over the redeemed world he has made.[6]

Worship in the New Creation

In Revelation 21, John's vision of the new creation is recorded:

Then I saw "a new heaven and a new earth," for the first heaven and the first earth had passed away, and there was no longer any sea. I saw the Holy City, the new Jerusalem, coming down out of heaven from God, prepared as a bride beautifully dressed for her husband. And I heard a loud voice from the throne saying, "Look! God's dwelling place is now among the people, and he will dwell with them. They will be his people, and God himself will be with them and be their God. 'He will wipe every tear from their eyes. There will be no more death' or mourning or crying or pain, for the old order of things has passed away." He who was seated on the throne said, "I am making everything new!" Then he said, "Write this down, for these words are trustworthy and true." (vv. 1–5)

These words depict the Holy City as a beautiful bride stunningly adorned for her groom. Have you ever attended a wedding and almost had your breath taken away when you

---

[6] N. T. Wright, "Heaven Is Not Our Home," *Christianity Today*, March 24, 2008, http://www.christianitytoday.com/ct/2008/april/13.36.html.

turned and saw the bride making her way down the aisle to meet her groom? The elegance of the Holy City is exponentially more beautiful. And before John can catch his breath, he hears a voice crying out: "God is dwelling with God's people; they will be his people, and he will be their God." These are words of promise that God made to Israel in generations past; now these covenantal words, "You will be my people and I will be your God," encompass people from every tongue, tribe, and time.

Missiologist Lesslie Newbiggin once said, "Jesus didn't write a book; Jesus formed a community." This gathering of redeemed people is an assembly of men and women, boys and girls who will relate to one another and our Savior forever and ever. This is the new community of the redeemed; and within this people, there will be no more death or grief, as these things belong to the old order, not the new creation. And this glorious God who rules and reigns over the whole of creation is also making all things new. Notice the text does not say God is making all new things. In the new creation there will be a renewal of everything—a continuity between what was, what is, and what is to come.

When the kingdom comes in its fullness, we will continue to worship by offering our lives back to God for the life of the beloved community. Yes, we will sing songs of adoration and thanksgiving. Yes, we will live in perfect harmony and peace with God, one another, and the whole of creation. Yes, we will engage in work, and our work will not only glorify God, but will be a source of joy to the beloved community as well. And yes, we will feast.

Remember the incredible vision of the new creation that was described by the prophet Isaiah? This was a vision filled with worship, community, and a magnificent table:

On this mountain the Lord Almighty will prepare
  a feast of rich food for all peoples,
a banquet of aged wine—
  the best of meats and the finest of wines.
On this mountain he will destroy
  the shroud that enfolds all peoples,
the sheet that covers all nations;
  he will swallow up death forever.
The Sovereign Lord will wipe away the tears
  from all faces;
he will remove his people's disgrace
  from all the earth.
The Lord has spoken.

In that day they will say,
"Surely this is our God;
  we trusted in him, and he saved us.
This is the Lord, we trusted in him; let us rejoice
  and be glad in his salvation." (Isaiah 25:6–9)

In this fractured world, we weep with those who weep, brushing aside tears now, in anticipation of the day when God will wipe away every tear and death is swallowed up by life. We do justice, love mercy, and walk humbly with God now, upholding the dignity of all people, in anticipation of the day when God will remove every vestige of shame, guilt, and disgrace. We share the good news of Jesus' life, death, and resurrection with people now, in anticipation of the day when all God's people will say, "This is our God. We trusted him. Let us rejoice and be glad in our salvation." And we feast now, in anticipation of the great day when all God's people will gather around the table, celebrating the reality that all things are as they ought to be.

So come to the table now; taste and see how good God really is. And offer your life back to God for the life of the world.

acknowledgements

This book has been a work of heart, and over the course of the project I have been fortunate to connect with many incredible people. My hope was not only to write a book, but also to nurture a community of people who would share this journey with me. That prayer has become a reality as this project has reminded me of the power of friendship and collaborative relationships.

The essence of this book was first communicated in a teaching series in our community of faith. Christ Community Church of the South Hills is a community of men and women, boys and girls who take seriously God's invitation to feast, and it is a privilege to share the journey of life together.

Thank you to my Indiegogo supporters for your belief in me and your investment in the project. A special thanks to: Deb Antonucci, Dawn Begor, Dave Bindewald, Merritt Blake, Chris and Joella Cavell, Patrick Colleti, Brad and Carole Craft, Jim and Laura Donahoe, Brad Fisher, Darrin Grove, Sue Hutchins, Gary and Natalie Kammeraad, Josh Kammeraad, Tadd and Joy

Laughlin, Terry Marshall, Mike McGreevy, Vinetia McGreevy, Leanne Meyer, Marilyn Mulvihill, Matt and Michelle Pruitt, Sue Puhala, Doug and Laurie Rabeneck, Nancy Rabold, Mark Ratti, Richie Reeder, Andy and Stacie Rhodes, Rich and Carol Shehab, Katherine Sikma, Lisa Slayton, Doug and Carin Smith, Greg and Jan Smith, Ken and Amy Smith, Greg and Amber Steele, Brent and Cara Thomas, Bob and Marvel Timm, Rob and Perity Timm, Joe and Margie Veltri, and Ken and Pennie Walters. I couldn't have done it without you.

Thank you to all who allowed me to share your stories. The way you offer your lives to God and to others inspires and motivates me.

I am grateful to Greg and Jan Smith as well as Ken and Amy Smith for their gifts of hospitality. Much of this book was written in the beautiful settings of Deep Creek Lake and Lake Latonka and having the keys and codes to your homes unlocked something within me.

Phil Mollenkof did an amazing job creating the cover art for the book. I appreciate his patience ("can we try one more thing, Phil?") and his ability to take the vision for this book and bring it to life in a compelling way.

As important as her editorial work was to this project, without Dianne Polome's encouragement, this book would not have become a reality. Dianne's feedback, questions, and comments made me a better writer and helped me tell a better story.

Thank you to my family, especially my wife Patty, for creating the space and granting me the grace to write. I am grateful for the years that we have been able to feast together and for the joy of doing life together.

Most of all, I want to thank the One who made a place at the table for me to feast. The mercy and grace that I have experienced through Jesus Christ has enabled me to taste and see how good God really is.

study guide: feasting together

Have you ever noticed how a good meal can be transformed into a great meal through the conversation and interaction that takes place when friends and family gather around the table? As people recall the events of their day, share their joys and their sorrows, and their successes and their failures, an ordinary meal can become a glorious feast.

This guide is designed for use by a small group of friends assembled around a kitchen table or a space in your favorite coffee shop or café. The questions are intended to facilitate conversation and help you explore the primary themes of the book; and as you press into the content together, my prayer is that God will make much of the ideas I have shared. I trust that the questions will serve you well, but if they do not, feel free to discard them and create your own.

As you gather together around the table, may you experience a foretaste of the kingdom, taste and see how good God really is, and more fully offer your lives back to God for the life of the world.

Introduction and Chapter One: Taste and See

When and where have you experienced the goodness of God? Do your best to describe as many details as you can remember. What did it look like, smell like, feel like, taste like, and sound like?

Reflect upon the three questions and quote from N. T. Wright (page 17) and share your responses: What is the most beautiful thing you experienced this week? What does this beauty do to you? What does this beauty call out of you?

What is the relationship between beauty, awe, reverence, and worship?

Chapter Two: An Invitation to Feast

What are your background and experiences with liturgy? What comes to mind when you hear the word "liturgy"?

How does the Gregorian calendar shape your life? How does the liturgical calendar shape your life? In what ways do these two calendars form and inform your spiritual journey?

On pages 25–28, the triune God—Father, Son, and Holy Spirit—is described using the image of the Divine Dance. How does this image inform your understanding of God? In what ways does a Trinitarian perspective of God shape the way you not only view worship, but also participate in worship?

How does the phrase "here is the new there" impact the way you look at the work of God in the world today and the opportunities you have to experience and engage in worship?

Chapter Three: What Is Worship?

Pop worship is a way of life that encompasses the everyday, ordinary things of life (page 39). In what ways is this true of your own life?

Work through the various descriptions of worship in this chapter. What are the strengths and weaknesses of each of them?

What place have the sacraments had in your practice of worship? Share your thoughts on a sacramental approach to worship. What is the difference between participating in the sacraments of corporate worship and participating in a sacramental life of worship?

In what ways does Jesus model for you a life of worship?

Chapter Four: Worship and Mission

In what ways is worship a "dangerous" activity?

Describe the *missio dei*. What comes to your mind as you consider the idea that God is a missional God?

Stuart Murray talks about God's mission being "cosmic in scope." What does that mean to you? How large is your understanding of the redemptive work of Jesus Christ? In what ways does salvation extend beyond the individual forgiveness of sins?

What would it look like to take the lid off your life this week? Share some possibilities, and pray for one another as you step out and join God in God's redemptive mission.

Chapter Five: Worship as Work

In what ways do you resonate with Donald Miller's experience of corporate worship? What points of tension do his words create in your mind?

How and where do you best connect with God?

Which of the three E's (education, entertainment, or experience) have most influenced your understanding and participation in worship? Describe the ways this has happened.

Liturgy is the "work of the people." How do liturgical practices inside the walls of the church shape you? What about cultural liturgies? Describe a cultural liturgy that has had an impact upon your life.

The Hebrew word *avodah* brings together our work, worship, and service. How does this enlarge and expand your understanding and practice of worship? Share some specific examples from the various dimensions of your life that can be informed by the practice of avodah.

In what ways does your worship make the world a more beautiful place?

Chapter Six: Worship in a Fractured World

Are you more of an optimist or pessimist?

How familiar are you with the practice of lament? Is it acceptable to question God or demand a response from God in the midst of pain, suffering, and oppression?

Where do you most experience the brokenness and gaps between the ways things are and the way things ought to be?

In the midst of a fractured world, what's right about your world?

Chapter Seven: Worship and Justice

Define justice. In what ways is justice in the world connected to the character and nature of God? What are the causes of injustice in our world?

Andrew Purves describes mercy and compassion as God's womb-like love. Does this image speak to you? How so? How does it feel to speak about God's mercy in feminine terms?

Has your life ever been "wrecked"? Describe the situation and circumstances. What pain and injustice in the world causes pain in your gut?

What can you learn from Jesus' example of humility? In what ways have you perhaps misunderstood what humility means? How does C. S. Lewis' statement, "Humility isn't thinking less of yourself; humility is thinking of yourself less" impact the way you live?

In what ways can you take up the challenge of Micah in your everyday, ordinary life?

Chapter Eight: Worship in the New Creation

How do you describe heaven? What has shaped your viewpoint and perspective?

Walk through the grand narrative of salvation history. Briefly summarize the four chapters (Creation, Fall, Redemption, and Restoration) in your own words.

Jesus said the kingdom of God is at hand. In what ways is the kingdom already here? In what ways is it yet to come?

N. T. Wright stated that God's goal was not to "snatch people away from earth to heaven but to colonize earth with the life of heaven." What does this mean to you? What does it look like to join God in making the petition from the Lord's Prayer "on earth as it is in heaven" a reality?

In what ways will your work of worship continue into the kingdom when it comes in its fullness?

an everyday, ordinary liturgy

L iturgy forms and shapes us. There is a Latin phrase, *lex orandi, lex credendi, lex vivendi* that is often translated "as we worship, so we believe, so we live." The prayers we pray, the songs we sing, and the activities and actions of worship—they shape us and form us in conscious and subconscious ways.

Liturgy occurs both inside the walls of the church during corporate worship and outside the walls of the church in our everyday, ordinary lives. C. S. Lewis wrote about the power of liturgy to turn our attention to God (and isn't that essential to worship?):

> *And it enables us to do these things best—if you like, it "works" best—when, through long familiarity, we don't have to think about it. As long as you notice, and have to count the steps, you are not yet dancing but only learning to dance. A good shoe is a shoe you don't notice. Good reading becomes possible when you need not*

consciously think about eyes, or light, or print, or spelling. The perfect church service would be one we were almost unaware of; our attention would have been on God.[1]

I have taken six common elements of corporate worship, reframed them, and shared some ideas that help me take my worship beyond the walls of the sanctuary and into the world. Try these practices on for size. Feel free to edit and adapt them as you see fit, or set them aside completely and try something different. Whatever you do, ask the Spirit of God today to help you do the work of worship in the places you live, learn, work, serve, and play.

The Call to Worship

Worship gatherings typically begin with a call to worship. It may be a song, a Scripture reading, or a prayer. Some churches use bells, chimes, or some other instrumental sound. Whatever the form, the call to worship serves as a signal, a reminder, and a focal point alerting the gathered that the activity of worship is set to begin.

I like what Chris Gambill says:

The call to worship is a tool to remind us about God. About who He is. About His unchanging character. About His love, grace, faithfulness, majesty, and might. It reminds us that we only come into God's presence because He has invited us through the blood of Jesus

---

[1] C. S. Lewis, *Letters to Malcolm: Chiefly on Prayer* (Harcourt Books: San Diego, 2002), 4.

Christ. And in that invitation, because of who God is, we are invited to worship Him as His people."[2]

What wakes you up in the morning? An alarm clock? Your phone? Birds sweetly singing or children noisily preparing for school? Whatever your wake-up call may be, welcome it and allow it to become a prompt for worship. As your eyes open and you become aware of the breath filling your lungs, let your first thoughts be directed toward God.

Commit your day to the Lord, consecrate yourself afresh, and through Christ, offer your everyday, ordinary life as an act of worship.

An Affirmation of Faith

In corporate worship, the people of God affirm their faith by declaring an historic confession of the Christian faith like the Apostles Creed or Nicene Creed or through the proclamation of a more contemporary expression of faith. These affirmations connect us with the one, holy, catholic church; and as we declare them, we give testimony to what we know and believe to be true, right, and good.

In Philippians 4, the Apostle Paul writes: "Finally, brothers and sisters, whatever is true, whatever is noble, whatever is right, whatever is pure, whatever is lovely, whatever is admirable—if anything is excellent or praiseworthy—think about such things" (Philippians 4:8).

Today in your everyday, ordinary life, find opportunities to not only think about the kinds of things Paul mentions in

[2] Chris Gambill, "How the Call to Worship Fosters God-Focused Worship," *Journey of Worship*, (blog), http://www.journeyofworship.com/2012/how-the-call-to-worship-fosters-god-focused-worship/.

Philippians 4, but affirm them as well. Whenever you see something good, true, or beautiful, take note of it. Ponder it, reflect upon it. And affirm it.

Build the language of affirmation into your life. Point out the good, true, and beautiful things wherever you find them. Learn to declare: "That's true, that's noble, that's right, pure, lovely, and admirable … I affirm it."

A Prayer of Confession

Prayers of confession are opportunities to come clean before God, to open up our lives to the One who already knows us inside and out. The word confession means to "agree with." When the people of God confess their sins, they are, in a sense, coming into agreement with God about their state of sinfulness.

John Ortberg says that a sinner's favorite prayer is "Lord, don't watch me now."

There is a rich tradition of prayers of confession in the Scriptures. Perhaps the best example is found in the prayer of David as recorded in Psalm 51: "For I know my transgressions, and my sin is always before me. Against you, you only, have I sinned and done what is evil in your sight; so you are right in your verdict and justified when you judge. Surely I was sinful at birth, sinful from the time my mother conceived me" (Psalm 51:1–3).

The Anglican tradition includes this prayer of confession in its *Book of Common Prayer*:

> *Most merciful God, we confess that we have sinned against you in thought, word, and deed, by what we have done, and by what we have left undone. We have not loved you with our whole heart; we have not loved our neighbors as ourselves. We are truly sorry and we*

*humbly repent. For the sake of your Son Jesus Christ,
have mercy on us and forgive us; that we may delight in
your will, and walk in your ways, to the glory of your
Name. Amen.*

Take a few moments to scan the headlines. More often than
not, they are dominated by bad news rather than good news.

Instead of being quick to judge others, take an opportunity to
examine your own heart. The truth is, the bad news is not only
out there; it's inside each of us and all of us. As God reveals the
sinfulness of your heart, use this ancient prayer: "Lord Jesus
Christ, Son of God, have mercy on me."

As your day comes to a close, take a few moments to scroll
through your day. In what ways have you failed to love God with
your whole heart? In what ways have you failed to love your
neighbor, your spouse, your co-workers, and others as yourself?

Examine your heart with the words from Psalm 139:23–24:
"Search me, God, and know my heart; test me and know my
anxious thoughts. See if there is any offensive way in me, and lead
me in the way everlasting."

The Passing of the Peace

The passing of the peace is a tradition that has deep roots in
Scripture. After his resurrection, Jesus greeted his disciples with
the words, "Peace be with you" (John 20:19). The Apostle Paul
typically began his letters with the greeting, "Grace and peace to
you from God the Father and the Lord Jesus Christ."

The passing of the peace embodies our identity as children of
God and also our call from Jesus to be peacemakers. As well, this
piece of the liturgy conditions and trains our hearts, hands, and
tongues in the ways of peace.

In more formal settings, the people of God rise from their seats and pronounce these words to their fellow worshippers: "The peace of Christ be with you. And also with you." In less formal settings, people will greet one another with high fives, hugs, and perhaps even a holy kiss.

As you walk through your office, school, or neighborhood, lift up your head, and be proactive to make eye contact with people, greeting them by name. And while saying, "The peace of Christ be with you" may not be appropriate in every setting, a simple "Peace be with you" might brighten someone's day or open up an opportunity for further conversation.

Offering

"The Christian life is marked by the offering of one's self to God to be shaped, empowered, directed, and changed by God. In worship, God presents us with the costly self-offering of Jesus Christ. We are claimed by Christ and set free. In response to God's love in Jesus Christ, we offer God our lives, our gifts, our abilities, and our material goods, for God's service." (*The Book of Common Worship*)

Earlier in the book, I introduced you to one of my favorite Hebrew words, *avodah*. In some places avodah is translated "work"; in other places it is translated as "worship," and still other times as "serve."

David Miller, in his introduction to Dorothy Sayer's essay "Why Work," writes, "This rich, biblical, and integrated concept of avodah provides the understanding of work through which we both worship God and serve neighbor."

I love the way Eugene Peterson captures the words of the Apostle Paul in his letter to the church in Rome: "So here's what I want you to do, God helping you: Take your everyday, ordinary life—your sleeping, eating, going-to-work, and walking-around life—and place it before God as an offering" (Romans 12:1, *The Message*).

Workers, what would it look like for you to place your work before God as an offering? Here are a few ideas:

- What tools do you use in your work? As you begin your workday, physically lift them up and consecrate them in worship to God and service to others.

- Before you present a completed project to a supervisor or client, offer the work of your hands to God, and ask God to use your work to promote the common good and flourishing of others.

- In what ways can you open up space in your workplace for others to engage in meaningful work?

Parents, what would it look like for you to place your parenting before God as an offering? Here are a few ideas:

- Ponder and reflect on your child's uniqueness. How has God fearfully created your child? Allow those insights to stir up a sense of wonder within you, and thank the One who created your child and entrusted his or her care to you.

- Take a walk with your child, keeping in mind the words of Deuteronomy 6:6–7: "These commandments that I give you today are to be on your hearts. Impress them on your children. Talk about them when you sit at home and when you walk along the road, when you lie down and when you get up." How can your walk become a time of guidance and teaching?

Students, what would it look like for you to place your study before God as an offering? Here are a few ideas:

- Begin your studies by offering a prayer of gratitude, thanking God for the opportunity to learn and expand your knowledge base.
- Reflect on the activity of God in each discipline of study. Ask God to show you his fingerprints throughout your field.

In light of Colossians 3:23, "Whatever you do, work at it with all your heart, as working for the Lord, not for human masters," offer your best to God.

Benediction

The word benediction is derived from the Latin (*bene*, well + *dicere*, to speak), and its literal meaning is to speak a good word. Benedictions are typically pronounced at the end of a worship gathering. The pastor or worship leader may lift up his or her hands and speak a word of blessing over the people. (If this is the practice in your faith community, may I suggest that the next time the benediction is spoken, instead of closing your eyes and bowing your head, lift up your head and make eye contact with the One who blesses you).

Here are two of the most well-known Scriptural benedictions:

The LORD bless you and keep you; the LORD make his face shine on you and be gracious to you; the LORD turn his face toward you and give you peace. (Numbers 6:24–26)

May the grace of the Lord Jesus Christ, and the love of God, and the fellowship of the Holy Spirit be with you all. (2 Corinthians 13:14)

Throughout the day, look for opportunities to bless people by pronouncing a benediction upon them. Leverage technology to speak a good word into someone's life:

- Send a text message
- Post something to someone's Facebook wall
- Send a direct message via Twitter
- Or go old school and make a phone call

Do you know the names of the people who serve you throughout your day and week? For instance:

- The baristas at the local coffee shop
- Your postal carrier or delivery person
- The checkout person in the grocery store
- The crossing guard

Learn their names and then find ways to thank them. Make sure they know that you appreciate the work they do and the way they serve. Bless them!

My hope for this appendix is to help you make a connection between your Sunday worship and your everyday, ordinary life. I believe God's goal is that we would live integrated lives and that our worship would extend beyond the walls of the sanctuary into the places we live, learn, work, serve, and play.

What practices have you found helpful? How have you integrated these rituals into your daily routines and rhythms? What other ways have you connected your Sunday liturgy with your worship throughout the week? I would love to hear from you, and I value your feedback and input. You can email me at terry@terrytimm.com.

for further reading

2 Corinthians: Power in Weakness by Kent R. Hughes, Wheaton: Crossway Books, 2006.

The African Bible Commentary by Tokunboh Adeyemo, ed. Grand Rapids: Zondervan, 2006.

The Air I Breathe: Worship as a Way of Life by Louis Giglio, Colorado Springs: Multnomah Books, 2006.

The Artisan Soul by Erwin McManus, New York: HarperOne, 2014.

Church Planting: Laying Foundations by Stuart Murray, Scotdale: Herald Press, 2001.

The Dangerous Act of Worship: Living God's Call to Justice by Mark Labberton, Downers Grove: InterVarsity Press, 2007.

Ecstasy and Intimacy: When the Holy Spirit Meets the Human Spirit by Edith Humphrey, Grand Rapids: Wm. B. Eerdmans Publishing Company, 2005.

Experiential Worship: Encountering God with Heart, Soul, Mind and Strength by Bob Rognlien, Colorado Springs: NavPress, 2005.

For the Life of the World: Sacraments and Orthodoxy by Alexander Schmemann, Yonkers: St. Vladimir's Seminary Press, 1997.

Good to Great: Why Some Companies Make the Leap and Others Don't by James Collins, New York: Harper Business, 2001.

Grace Eventually: Thoughts on Faith by Anne Lamott, New York: Riverhead Trade, 2007.

How Long, O Lord: Reflections on Suffering and Evil by D. A. Carson, Grand Rapids: Baker Academic, 2006.

Integrity: The Courage to Face the Demands of Reality by Henry Cloud, New York: HarperCollins, 2006.

Letters to Malcolm: Chiefly on Prayer by C. S. Lewis, San Diego: Harcourt Books, 2002.

Liturgy as a Way of Life: Embodying the Arts in Christian Worship by Bruce Ellis Benson, Grand Rapids: Baker Publishing Group, 2013.

Love Wins: A Book About Heaven, Hell, and the Fate of Every Person Who Ever Lived by Rob Bell, New York: HarperOne, 2001.

The Message of the Psalms: A Theological Commentary by Walter Brueggeman, Minneapolis: Fortress Press, 1985.

Old Testament Theology: Essays on Structure, Theme and Text by Walter Brueggeman, Minneapolis: Augsburg Fortress, 1992.

Participating in God: A Pastoral Doctrine of the Trinity by Paul Fiddes, Louisville: Westminster John Knox Press, 2001.

The Search for Compassion: Spirituality and Ministry by Andrew Purves, Louisville: Westminster John Knox Press, 1989.

Surprised by Hope: Rethinking Heaven, the Resurrection and the Mission of the Church by N. T. Wright, New York: HarperOne, 2008.

The True Story of the Whole World: Finding Your Place in the Biblical Drama by Craig C. Bartholemew and Michael W. Goheen, Grand Rapids: Faith Alive Christian Resources, 2009.

When the Kings Come Marching In by Richard Mouw, Grand Rapids: Wm. B. Eerdmans, revised edition, 2002.

Worship Leaders, We Are Not Rock Stars by Stephen Miller, New York: Moody Publishers, 2013.

Worship Old and New by Robert Webber, Grand Rapids: Zondervan, 1994.

Worship, Community and the Triune God of Grace by James B. Torrance, Downers Grove: InterVarsity Press, 1997.

Wrecked: When a Broken World Slams into Your Comfortable Life by Jeff Goins, Chicago: Moody Press, 2012.

52976043R00102

Made in the USA
Middletown, DE
24 November 2017